THE DRUMMER OF MIAMI BEACH

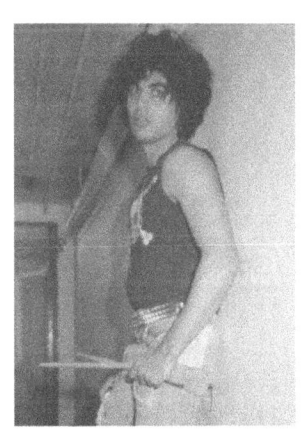

THE STORY OF JOEY WRECKED

THE DRUMMER OF MIAMI BEACH

JOEY MAYA

Jitney Books

The Drummer of Miami Beach by Joey Maya
Copyright © 2018

Published by Jitney Books

All rights reserved. No part of this book may be reproduced without the publisher's written permission, except for brief quotations in reviews.

Printed in the United States of America

Front cover art by Luis Berros
Jitney books logo by Ahol Sniffs Glue
Copy edited and lay out by J.J. Colagrande
Front cover design by Marlene Lopez
Author photos: Teajay Smith & Pepi Susi

Jitney Books is a Miami-based micro-publishing company focused on producing original titles by Miami-based authors writing about Miami in Miami with the intention of this material being produced into film or plays by Miami-based filmmakers or playwrights. All cover art will feature Miami-based artists.

All intellectual property rights remain with the artists and authors.

Please contact publisher for media, acquisition and collaboration inquiries:

jitneybooks@gmail.com

@jitneybooks

#MADEINDADE

#MIAMIFULLTIME

Music fans, this is the real story.

Musicians, you already know.

THE DRUMMER OF MIAMI BEACH

Table of Contents

Introduction 1
The Drummer 5
Miami Beach 9
The Reactions 18
The Meteoric Rise of The Reactions 22
Our First Record 31
A Jamaican Record Label to the Rescue…Yah Mon! 39
That's No Way to Spend Your Youth 43
The Reactions Love You 50
An Offer We Can't Refuse 57
Joey Goes to College 64
Black Flag and the Turnpike Killer 77
Paying Dues 85
New York City 95
Stayin' Alive in NYC 108
The Slums of South Beach 119
Finding Joey Wrecked 125
Battalion of Saints 131
Road Dogs 142
The End of the Road? 149
Punk Rock Winter 155
Shaka Brah…Dude 165
Battalion of Saints Do America 176
The Cornfields of Iowa and the Insane Asylum 193
Hello West Coast…Goodbye 197
Take Me Back to New York City 204
Circus of Power 210
Regrets…I've Had a Few 217
Dreams Tonight 223

Introduction

After performing at a concert in Kenosha, Wisconsin, my bandmates and I were hanging out backstage with a group of young autoworkers from the local plant. One of those autoworkers had just gotten out of jail that very same day and was very happy to be back with his beautiful 5'8" blonde girlfriend from Racine, who looked like she had stepped right out of a *Penthouse* magazine. She certainly did not fit my perception of what a girl from Racine, Wisconsin, an industrial town just 10 miles north of Kenosha, should look like. The boyfriend looked like the kind of guy who wasn't very worried about being in jail. So wisely, I barely even glanced at this absurdly hot girl. Truth be told, all of my bandmates and I were kind of intimidated by the plant workers hanging out with us that night, especially the guy who had just gotten out of jail. These guys worked all day building automobiles, and they looked it. We were happy-go-lucky, touring musicians, and that's what we looked like. They were giving us strange looks, and we all thought it was just a matter of when they were gonna beat the shit out of us, and not if. We were road hardened and had already been involved in our share of fracases, but these hard-working guys were like nothing we had seen on our tours of the East and West Coasts. This was the Midwest, the industrial heartland of America.

As the evening progressed, we ended up at a local bar not far from the house that we were all crashing at that night and drank **a lot** of beers together. Surprisingly, everybody turned out to be very friendly. At closing time, as we were walking back to the

Introduction

house, I somehow ended up next to the gorgeous blonde girl, and she unexpectedly declared she would come to my room as soon as her boyfriend, the guy fresh out of jail, fell asleep. I told her I really didn't think that was such a good idea, but she assured me once he passed out, there would be no waking him.

Walking with us was the guitar player, Chris Smith. Chris was a bona fide rock star. He was thin, blond, blue-eyed and fully tattooed. A real bad boy. He was a gifted guitar player and was constantly sought after by the biggest, best rock bands in the entire country. Musically, he was quite a few notches above me, and I felt very fortunate to share a stage with him. Chris really liked my playing, though, and if I was good enough for him, I was good enough to be in this band.

Chris was also a bona fide fucking mad man. He had overheard what she had said to me and was now trying to persuade this gift from the gods of porn themselves to knock on his door instead. He was stopping at nothing to convince her to choose him instead of me, including literally pointing out the outline of the obvious python in his black jeans. Normally that might have worked, and normally, I would have been pissed. But tonight, I was hoping he had convinced her.

We finally got back to the house where my room was a cluttered basement. Sure enough, 15 minutes later, there she was, striking a painfully sexy pose in my doorway. I couldn't resist. Within milliseconds, I made a conscientious, pro-active decision to risk my life to be with this girl. She was stunning! Figuring it was understood that given the circumstances, we were going for a quickie…I was quick all right. Immediately after, feeling spent and devilishly content, I told her how special she was and to look me up if we played in Wisconsin again.

Introduction

Well, the gorgeous young blonde had other ideas and was confident that I would rise again to meet them. She was certainly more confident than me. We had been slamming down beers since before the show had even started and stopped only after hearing the announcement of last call at the bar we ended at. My skinny, 162-pound frame was polluted with gallons of beer, so even though I was 22 years old and she was ridiculously hot, I just didn't think it would happen for me.

But then I started thinking; what if this chick, who was getting more and more vocal about her demands, freaked out and made a scene? I would be in a terrible pickle! It was either fuck her again, and this time do a better job of it, or risk a possible confrontation with a future habitual felon. Can you imagine? Thoughts of, "Honey, wake up. I decided to screw the drummer after you passed out, and he just didn't quite do it for me. Please murder him," floated in my head.

Talk about pressure! Inspired by what I had recently seen in the movie 9 ½ Weeks, I got some strawberries out of the fridge in the kitchen, which happened to be right next to the basement where I was staying. My lame plan was to be sensual with the strawberries long enough until I had recharged. Within a few very short minutes she started impatiently insisting that I stop teasing her. It was now or never, so I just went for it. Surprising even myself, I came through and fucked her like a champ, but this time, like a gentleman, I finished immediately **after** her (I was 22!). Firmly, but politely, I then asked this beautiful psycho to go back to her boyfriend. The next morning, my bandmates and I said goodbye to everyone who had slept over, including the blonde who was standing there holding hands with her jailbird boyfriend, and we left for Chicago.

Introduction

Guess who I ran into after the show in Chicago? The blonde. She had showed up with one of her girlfriends. Life on the road was awesome!

The Drummer

The drummer is the guy in the band who fucks your girlfriend. Who looks cool, acts like he doesn't give a shit, and girls are almost irrationally attracted to.

I am a drummer.

Undoubtedly, every guy wants to be that rebel who makes girls wet their panties. I mean **every** guy. It's the real reason we play sports, become musicians, ride motorcycles, and learn to write computer code. It's the real reason we do a lot of things.

But is a drummer just a cool cat that girls throw themselves at?

Certainly not.

As a matter of fact, drummers are the Rodney Dangerfields of musicians; they get no respect from the public and their own ego fueled band members often do not fully appreciate the influence a drummer can have on the band's success. The drummer can literally make or break a band. The difference between making millions of dollars each year playing sold-out concert halls, or playing only at the local pub on weekends, just might be the lowly fucking drummer. Obviously, if the band just altogether sucks, having Dave Grohl in the group won't change that. I'm guessing you understand my point.

My story however, is not about drummers; it's about me. It just so happens there are numerous similarities and parallels

The Drummer

between drumming and the adventures and challenges I've encountered. And of course, I really am a drummer.

It has been difficult for me to share my experiences openly with other people. In my day job, I help individual bond investors manage their municipal bond portfolios, so I am always on good behavior with my co-workers. My circle of friends is mostly from Temple Solel, a Jewish synagogue, and my stories of how wasted we were all of the time would be social suicide. I have two, young teenage daughters, and I'm afraid that the Jewish moms that we are friends with might not allow their kids to hang out with my kids if they knew about my crazy rock and roll past. To be fair, I was always the straight and responsible one of each of the bands I ever played in. But then again, also to be fair, the bar was set pretty low.

My wife certainly doesn't want to hear about the amorous fans that expressed their appreciation for the arts, or as she would probably phrase it, doesn't want to hear about the sluts I fucked in each city. My anecdotes would either be way out of line or might seem as if I was bragging. I have therefore mostly kept them to myself all these years.

The other side of the coin is also difficult; my musician friends don't understand how I could possibly live the (apparently) mundane life that I now live. How I can wake up every single day at 6 a.m. and put on a necktie before going to work at 7:30 a.m. It's like I crossed over to the dark side. My good buddy Captain Scarlet, who played with me in the band Battalion of Saints, was so flabbergasted that I was turning my back on rock and roll, that he dosed me with a hit of acid one hour before my first training session with the manager of the Wall Street firm that had hired me as a financial advisor. The manager, who was now in his early thirties and settled down, had done his share of

The Drummer

partying as a young man, and was instrumental in giving long-haired, rock and roll me an opportunity that I normally would not have had access to. Entering this brand-new world was difficult enough…but showing up tripping my balls off to the training session was fucking insane! I do not knowingly ever take hallucinogens, and I quit smoking pot when I was 18, so I was definitely not accustomed to mind altering drugs. Somehow, and I cannot recall with any clarity now, I did make it through that training session.

As angry as I was, I know why Scarlet did it; he wanted me to realize that this 180-degree change in my life was the wrong path for me. What I now do for a living couldn't be further from the world of rock and roll. It is especially difficult after having lived the life that I was living and receiving the special attention and favoritism that I was privy to. Rock and roll hours were also certainly more to my liking!

Therein lies the problem; I can't win. My friends that are not from the world of rock and roll think the worst anyway. They think that all I did was play music, take a bunch of drugs, drink a lot of alcohol, and sleep with a lot of different women. I'm not saying that wasn't true, but is that such a bad thing? Am I not allowed to talk about it? I hear **their** stories. And my stories are much better. Even so, I decided it would be better to keep absolutely quiet about my past rock and roll life.

Hopefully, after reading my story you'll have a deeper appreciation for the musicians that risk everything in order to stay in the music business. The very great majority of musicians will never make it "big." As a matter of fact, the great majority will never even be able to make a living as musicians.

The Drummer

But that doesn't mean our stories are any less interesting than the rock star that becomes a multi-millionaire and lives the rock and roll dream. We already know that story. I read, and enjoyed Keith Richard's book, but I knew the story; he listened to a lot of American rhythm and blues, got good at playing it on guitar, met Mick Jagger and started a great rock and roll band, did a butt load of drugs, became very rich, and said he had a bigger dick than Mick Jagger. We **all** know the story, and most of us don't care whose dick is bigger. What I am certain of is that you don't know the story of the guy or girl who has to continuously decide whether to quit or to continue their career in music, fully knowing that the deeper he or she gets, the harder it will be to ever recover if things don't work out as planned.

That, to me, is much more interesting.

Although all wannabe rock stars share a common thread, each individual has their own unique story. I believe my story certainly qualifies as unique.

I hope you enjoy it.

Miami Beach

In 1984, I joined the band Battalion of Saints in New York City. I know what you're probably thinking: how does a 21-year-old from Miami Beach get invited to join an up-and-coming national band, especially one about to embark on an East Coast tour.

After all, the world of rock and roll was totally unaware of the burgeoning, talent laden, original rock and roll scene that existed in South Florida from 1979-1984, so it's certainly a fair question.

The ominous titles of the two indie documentaries that chronicle the early 80's South Florida music scene, *Invisible Bands* and *Rock and a Hard Place: Another Night at the Agora*, say it all. South Florida had one of the most vibrant and talented young music scenes in the entire nation. We were waiting for the world to discover us, but it just never did.

Most of the musicians from that South Florida original music scene were somewhere between the ages of 17 and 23. At that age, society forces you to decide on a trajectory that will have a significant, even dramatic, effect on your life for many years to come. For the most part, sometime right around after high school ends, we **all** basically have to decide on what we are going to do for the rest of our lives. The obvious choices are to go to college, or to get a job and start paying bills. Becoming a rock star is typically not one of the choices. Your mom or dad will invariably tell you that it's okay to keep playing music, but to do so while you are in college or working at a full-time job.

Miami Beach

In theory, working or going to college while you play music in your spare time would appear to make sense. But in practice, not so much. Making it in the music business is a full-time job, and if you're not completely focused on it, the odds, which are long to begin with, drop even further. I say, if you are not going to dedicate 100% of your time to music, you're better off just going to college or learning a trade that you will be happy doing for the rest of your life, and think of music as a hobby, not as a career. I've seen too many talented musicians do a half-ass job at their jobs **and** at music careers. They end up not being successful at either. Unfortunately, you can't have it both ways.

On the other hand, if you decide to dedicate 100% of your time to music and end up failing at it, what will you have? You'll be left with nothing but the deep regret of having squandered that precious window of time that you had to attain a college education or to have learned a sustainable trade. A heavy price, and a heavy burden indeed.

Well, phrased like that, it seems like an easy choice: success and happiness…or possible utter doom and depression?

It's obviously not that cut and dry. Plenty of young musicians eventually go to college, start businesses, or learn trades that allow them to lead perfectly productive and normal lives. Many excellent musicians continue to have careers in the music business without ever becoming famous themselves. And some aspiring young musicians even go on to become world-renowned actors; Johnny Depp happened to be one of those talented 17-23-year-old musicians from the 1980's South Florida original music scene!

What is certain, however, is that you will never get back the years that you spend trying to make it. And years, not months, is what it will take…if you even make it at all. As time passes, the odds of becoming a lawyer, doctor, investment banker, etc., fade away. Not everybody wishes to go down that path anyway, but if you did, the door of opportunity would eventually close, which is a major price to pay. At age 17, I was already aware of those consequences, and I wanted choices! So, the summer that I turned 19, I enrolled at University of Florida. By the end of that summer, it was clear that I never actually had a choice; college was **not** an option for me. I had to pursue my musical dreams, regardless of the risk or consequences.

What happened between the ages of 17 and 18 and a half that so drastically altered my future? The Reactions…that's what happened. I had the honor and pleasure to be involved with arguably one of the greatest rock and roll bands that the world never got the chance to hear. A bittersweet, but nevertheless true, distinction. The Reactions changed my life forever. At the time, I was convinced The Reactions were the culmination of a musical odyssey that began when I was a young kid banging on soda cracker cans with T-shirts on top to serve as drums, and pot lids hung with string to serve as cymbals. Turns out, as you will discover, The Reactions were only the beginning of that journey.

Before a person can even play in a cool band, he or she must learn to play a musical instrument. And that isn't easy. Here's a news flash…nobody sits down at a piano or picks up a musical instrument for the first time and churns out a beautiful melody. Nobody! Sure, some people can be more musical, just as some people can be better at math or sports, but that doesn't mean that they can instantly play a musical instrument. It just means they might enjoy it a little more or progress a little faster. It takes a very, very long time to learn an instrument. Think of each step of mastering a musical instrument as climbing a difficult mountain. If you manage to climb that mountain right up to the top, you

Miami Beach

will be exhilarated, but you will also probably be exhausted. Your musical journey doesn't end there...it begins there. There will be many, many more difficult mountains left to conquer.

Most people try and relate the process of becoming a musician to something in their lives that they have managed to get really good at. But it doesn't make for a fair comparison. If you dedicate years and years of your life to becoming a great doctor or lawyer you already know ahead of time that you will be rewarded with extraordinary financial compensation and be very well respected in your community. And I say deservedly so. The difference is, musicians understand they are never likely to be financially rewarded for their mastery of a musical instrument and heck, oftentimes talented musicians are looked at contemptibly because they look or dress differently and are not financially stable. I believe it is important to appreciate what it took for the musician to turn the inanimate, cold object that is in their hands into a beautiful melody that brightens our day, and all of our lives. Next time you see a person playing a musical instrument at a subway stop in NYC or on a dingy, dirty sidewalk, don't disdainfully sneer at them. I'm not sure how they ended up in a dank underground subway or on that inhospitable sidewalk, but to play what they appear to be feeling, somewhere, sometime, they dedicated some serious hours to learning that instrument. Enjoy the music for a moment or until your train pulls up, and then give them a dollar or some frigging change. Trust me, the violin player in the subway, that cool rock star you see at a concert, and the guitar players at local pubs on weekends all started out as geeky musical students.

So yes, I was also a music nerd! My friends were the saxophone players, the clarinetists, the violinists and the flute players. They wore braces on their teeth and glasses on their noses. They were usually smart, well-intentioned, nice kids and I was proud to be

Miami Beach

in band camp with them. Just kidding, no band camp for me. But I did take a lot of music classes every semester from middle school on. My schedule during my last two years at Miami Beach Senior High (Beach High) included:

Period 1: Orchestra (Percussion)

Period 2: Jazz Band (Drummer)

Period 3: Symphony (1st clarinet, 2nd chair)

Period 5: Guitar Ensemble (I played classical guitar in the performing guitar ensemble)

Even during the few non-music courses I was required to take, I was constantly doing drum rudiments quietly on my thigh. Rudiments are played with two drumsticks and are the boring, repetitive patterns that form the building blocks of all drumming. There are 13 basic rudiments and 13 additional rudiments. I practiced all 26, all the time. Music, including clarinet and guitar, was what I spent the most amount of time on. I wanted to be the most knowledgeable and skilled musician I could possibly be, and not just a dumb drummer.

Outside of school, I played in garage bands. Even if I was playing with perfectly good musicians, if the opportunity came along to play with better players, I was gone. It sounds kind of cutthroat, but it was understood that's just how it was, and that's just what I did to get better.

My goal was to form a great band, and a drummer, more so than any other instrument, is highly dependent on the other players in the group. It dawned on me early-on that as a drummer, my destiny was closely tied to the songwriters of the band, and to

Miami Beach

how well the guitar players and singers played and sang the songs. Simply put, without good songs and good musicians, a band will not be successful. Therefore, I always looked to align myself with great songwriters. As far as singers and guitar players were concerned, I knew what was good enough and what wasn't. A singer doesn't have to have the vocal range of Roy Orbison but must hit the notes that he or she attempts. Nothing turns people off quicker than a few sour notes from the singer's lips. The guitar player also needs not be Jeff Beck, but at least talented enough to play complex changes cleanly and to sound exciting and creative. What I brought to the table was the ability to help those well-written, well-played songs sound great by complimenting them with my drumming and overall music skills. These are intangible qualities that can't be overemphasized. A drummer that is even very talented and skillful can literally ruin a song by over-playing it or just not playing it right.

My task, therefore, was to not only improve my own drumming abilities, but to find players that I had chemistry with so that my good musical taste would help shape the sound of the band. I was never interested to be a drummer for hire, because frankly speaking, there were thousands of drummers in music schools all over the country, and probably just as many who were not in schools, with better technical skills than me. No, I wanted to be Keith Moon or Charlie Watts; drummers whose distinctive styles of playing were synonymous with the sound of their respective bands. I'm not saying The Who or The Rolling Stones needed Moon or Watts more than Moon or Watts needed them. But I am absolutely saying that neither band would be the same without them. I needed to find my own Who or Rolling Stones.

At the same time that I was looking for my own band, my own Pete Townshend, Isaac Baruch was looking for his Keith Moon.

Miami Beach

From the first time we jammed together…Isaac playing his Les Paul at ear-splitting decibels while I banged away at my vintage Slingerland drum kit, the connection was obvious. It was clear that we were meant to be together.

I first met Isaac after I had miserably failed a Rock Ensemble audition during my junior year of high school. Rock Ensemble was the award-winning, rock music performing ensemble at Beach High. I was already the drummer of the high school's performing jazz band and the percussionist of the orchestra, so I figured it was foregone conclusion that Rock Ensemble would be honored to have me as well.

Turns out the audition proved otherwise. I was terrible! The band director, Doug Burris, asked each of the drummers auditioning to play a slow 6/8 time beat, and then he followed by asking us to play a 5/4 time beat. Those obscure, seldom used time signatures were rarely encountered in any songs, and most rock drummers, me included, wouldn't even have bothered to learn them. For the life of me, I didn't understand why the Rock Ensemble drummer should be chosen on the basis of such non rock and roll criteria. In retrospect, obscure time signatures aside, I wasn't the best drummer auditioning that day, and so I wasn't chosen to be the next drummer of Rock Ensemble.

When I left that room with my head spinning from the horrific audition, Isaac was waiting for me in the hallway. He introduced himself and asked me if I wanted to play in a band with him. I had heard good things about Isaac, so I said sure, that I would like that. Turns out that Isaac was a major upgrade to the guys I had been jamming with. Ironically, we then recruited the talented bass player of the Rock Ensemble, Mark Meland, and along with Jimmy Hendrix playing, surfer-dude Larry Burgos, we started ourselves a garage cover band that kicked-ass! We

Miami Beach

played James Gang, Aerosmith, MC5, Cheap Trick and just a ton of cool stuff that Rock Ensemble would never have played. It was fun and we sounded great, but after six months of playing together, we decided that our futures were not in playing other people's songs, and so we drifted apart. I stayed busy doing regular high school things and playing shortstop on the baseball team, but the music bug was now firmly imbedded in me.

Before that same junior year had even finished, I was already trying to reunite with Isaac, who had now formed a power pop group with fellow Beach Highers, singer/songwriter Tony Suppa and drummer Richie Weisbach. Richie was an outstanding drummer who over the years had often taken the time to share many helpful drumming tips with me.

After hearing Isaac's new band at the Irish House Bar and Grill on 14th street and Alton Road on Miami Beach, I knew right then and there…**that** was the music I wanted to play. I loved it…it was poppy, catchy, and energetic. Isaac and Tony had massive potential, and I wanted to be a part of it. I immediately asked Isaac if I could be in the band. His answer of course was that they already had a drummer, Richie. I remained persistent, even obnoxious, until finally a few months later, by the start of my senior year, Isaac relented and let me join the group. Sorry Richie and thank you for the many excellent drumming tips!

I believed that I was the missing piece that Isaac and Tony needed to take their music to the next level. It turns out I was partially right; I was **one** of the missing pieces that they needed. October and November of 1979, we worked on our original songs and we rehearsed. We knew that we needed a bass player who shared our vision, so that's what we focused on, finding that 4th piece of the puzzle.

Miami Beach

A solution presented itself when we heard through the grapevine that another local band's guitar player might be looking to join a second band. The Girls, a well-respected rock band, had a regular gig at a dive bar in Miami Beach near to where we practiced at in Surfside. Isaac came up with the ingenious idea to ask their guitar player if he would switch from lead guitar to bass guitar and join us. We had nothing to lose by asking, so after rehearsal one night, Isaac and I went and watched The Girls play their set. These guys were so much better musicians than us! Naturally, I thought the guitar player, the infamous Johnny "Too Bad" Salton, was gonna laugh in Isaac's face. But he didn't. It turned out Johnny was tired of playing Zeppelin and Heart. He was tired of playing what we now refer to as classic rock and wanted to try his hand at the nascent punk sounds that had reached our shores from England. Without even hearing us play, on the spot, Johnny Salton agreed to be our bass player.

Two things happened that night: The Reactions were born, and my life took a turn that would forever alter my future.

The Reactions

With the addition of Johnny Salton, we now had a complete band and were excited to hear what it was going to sound like. An hour before our first rehearsal practice, Isaac taught Johnny three of our original songs, which were relatively simple to learn on bass guitar.

I counted off the first song, and we ran through the three songs at our rehearsal space, which happened to be the guest bedroom of Isaac's mother, Carmen's, house. When we were done, Tony, Isaac, and I looked at each other as if to say, "That was fucking awesome!"

Then Johnny started to speak. "Um, that was great," he said to me quietly, as if he was being polite in sharing our enthusiasm, but had a slightly different opinion.

"Really powerful…but could you try it again with less fills?"

Drumming is basically composed of keeping a steady rhythm on the drum kit, and then filling, or playing interesting rolls and patterns, to usher in the next section of the song. A drummer's most important job is to keep a steady beat. Imagine if you were bopping along to a song, really digging it, and then all of a sudden the groove of the song disappeared. It would be very distracting, and if those interruptions were to continue, you would eventually lose all interest in the song. When a song calls for a little oomph, the drummer can add accents, even adding a short fill right before the accents. Those little fills and accents,

The Reactions

done creatively and tastefully, make the music more exciting and do not take away from the steady drive of the song. Great fills can turn a good song into a great song. Johnny wanted me to keep the beat, but to fill less. He wanted me to play accents, but he didn't want me going all "Buddy Rich" (one of the greatest jazz drummers of all time, who never passed on a chance to play a tasteful, powerful, short fill before hitting an accent). I gave him a smirking glance before we played the song again.

After the song was finished, Johnny came over to stand right next to me and a bit more forcibly this time said, "Joey, could you play even less fills?"

"Johnny, I barely even played any fills that time," I irritably complained!

"No, no…you sounded great. Your beat is really powerful. Just fill less and keep the beat steadier."

Johnny was much more experienced than any of us. He was 23 years old, basically an old man. So I was willing to listen to him.

I counted it off again and played the whole song with less fills.

"That was great!" he said approvingly. "The beat has to really drive the song, not distract it."

It didn't take long for me to realize that he was right. The songs were now sounding more like songs rather than endless jams. We finished rehearsal by playing the songs again, and this time recording them onto a cassette tape. Johnny and I listened to the songs in my car on the drive back to the Miami Beach Motel in the alley on 84th Street and Collins Avenue, where Johnny stayed with his dancer girlfriend, Denise.

The Reactions

Oh Denise! Denise, who always had to be the center of everyone's attention, was a lot of fun and truly a delightful sweetheart. It was really cool to be a 17-year-old high school student hanging out with a stripper and a 23-year-old guitar player who smoked a lot of pot and never had more than $20 in his pocket. I led a *Leave it to Beaver* like existence at school and at baseball practice until 6 p.m., and then went to hang out with Johnny and Denise. Fun! However, there is a serious dark side to the exotic dancing profession and eventually it became difficult to ignore the ugliness that came with the fun. Between the drugs, alcohol, and degenerates that abound at strip clubs, it is hardly a sustainable lifestyle. To Denise's credit, she always had a smile on her face and did her best to turn the lemons that were constantly falling on her, into lemonade. Denise cheerfully welcomed us into the deco inspired, cheap motel room. Johnny lit up a joint and then played the three songs again. He seemed to be grimacing whenever Isaac's guitar solos came up. I, on the other hand, **loved** Isaac's guitar solos. He rocked it!

In 1979, every song had a guitar break in it. It's the part of the song where there is no singing and the lead guitar player does a guitar solo above the music playing. You know, it's when the guitar player saunters over to the front of the stage like a rock god and jams out a guitar lead. We've all done that in front of a mirror, so don't pretend you don't know what I'm talking about.

"I don't think Isaac should be playing hard rock guitar solos over our power pop songs," Johnny semi-muttered as the joint dangled from his lips.

"Good luck convincing Isaac that his beloved guitar leads didn't fit in with our songs," I thought to myself.

The Reactions

The next day at rehearsal, Johnny asked Isaac to exchange his hard rock guitar solos, for melodic, tasteful leads.

Isaac gave Johnny the same smirking glance I had given him one day earlier, and said "Really?"

"Yes, Isaac. These are pop songs. Your hard rock leads don't belong in them. Why don't we try it?" he politely, almost sheepishly, asked.

We then played the first song. No drum fills, no electric guitar leads; just a freight train of driving beat and bass underpinning a beautiful melody, punctuated by tasteful guitar riffs and layered with anthem-like lyrics about love, disenchantment and rebellion. When the song was over, we didn't yell hooray or anything like that; it was more of a subdued, respectful, **holy shit**! We knew there was something special about what we had just done. It was totally original. We did not sound like anything that was out there. We were powerful and rough, but all of our melodies were catchy, sugary, and Beatles-like.

Very quickly, our gut-feelings would be confirmed. In three months, we went from Carmen's guest room to headlining The Agora Ballroom. Within four months of that first rehearsal, we were splashed on the front cover of the *Sun Sentinel Weekend Sunshine* section. There was a giant picture of our band! We seemingly had appeared out of nowhere and critics openly debated whether we were even ready for this kind of spotlight. But we were here to stay. All this was happening while I was still a senior at Miami Beach Senior High School. A few months earlier, I had quit the baseball team to concentrate on the music. My life was changing very, very quickly. Soon after the *Sun Sentinel* cover, I dropped out of high school altogether.

The Meteoric Rise of The Reactions

A meteor is a super bright light that whizzes by at an incredible speed, then explodes and disappears forever. That was The Reactions. Thank God we recorded a few records before we "exploded," so we won't ever be gone forever. If you have a pile of money to spend on a seven-inch Reactions record (the four-song *The Reactions Love You* currently goes for well over $400), you can add a Reactions record to your collection. But for all practical purposes, The Reactions disappeared a long time ago.

The Reactions played their first gig at the basement club of the Blue Waters Hotel on 74th Street and Ocean Terrace Drive on Miami Beach. The seedy hotel was on a dangerous block full of derelicts and nefarious characters hawking guns, drugs and hookers. If you go now, you will find a tall, shiny, luxury condominium. Back then, it was the perfect setting for dirty rock and roll. Johnny Salton had only been practicing with us for three weeks, but we decided to go for it anyway, and booked a Friday and a Saturday night.

As mature and hip as I fancied myself compared to the other kids in my high school, in reality I was still a naive high school jock and was totally unprepared to step into the world of adult, fucked up, crazy, Sex Pistols loving punk rockers.

It was our first public show and we had zero publicity for it. This was before social media, and there existed a real possibility that nobody but a few drunks or drug dealers would be in

The Meteoric Rise of The Reactions

attendance. But people did show up that Friday. What ensued was surreal, but indicative of what the next few years of our lives would be like. The bedlam, violence, and passion exhibited that night are the hallmarks of punk rock. It took me a while, but eventually I got used to it, and even grew to appreciate it.

There might have been thirty punk rockers at the club that Friday night. As soon as we started playing, they all started moshing wildly. Maybe it's common now, but in 1980, moshing was a relatively new phenomenon. The people in charge of security at the Blue Waters didn't understand what was going on and started trying to quell the crowd in a not very nice manner. Hell, none of us in the band knew what was going on either, but these people were there to see us, and we weren't going to let anybody push our "fans" around. Needless to say, it got a little ugly, but we played our set. When it was over, it was like we had ingested a powerful opiate. We were ecstatically high and instantly addicted to the rush. This is why people risk it all to be famous in the arts; it is an indescribable feeling. We may have gotten a little ahead of ourselves by extrapolating 30 rabid punk fans into international wealth and fame, just a little, but I'm telling you, that was what Isaac, Tony, Johnny, and I felt. I played in front of some large crowds after that, but that night and that feeling remains forever etched into my mind.

If Friday was wild, the next night, as more people heard about our band, was epic. I'm not sure how so many people found out about us. We were truly unknown, and the show was not publicized in any way whatsoever, but Saturday night, the small bar was packed solid.

We anonymously made our way through the crowd to take our places on the tiny stage at the far end of the club and then blasted through the set. Johnny was still making mistakes, as he

The Meteoric Rise of The Reactions

hadn't had enough time to learn every song yet. But mistakes and all, it was a powerful performance. I felt an energy coursing through my body that I had never felt before. I was playing crisper, faster, and stronger than I had ever played. The adrenaline transformed me into an animal behind the drums. I didn't know it then, obviously, but that Superman feeling would come back almost every time I played live shows. I expected, even counted upon that energy to help me play difficult sets to the best of my abilities.

Reaction songs were straightforward, melodic, catchy songs played at a very fast speed. Think Green Day dusted with a little bit of crystal meth. Our songs were played at a speed that hovered around 200 beats per minute, and even faster. For the sake of comparison, The Ramones played most of their songs at around 180 beats per minute, and they were by far one of the fastest bands around. There are two ways for a drummer to play at that speed. The easy way is to play two beats on the hi-hat for every one on the snare drum. The drummer of The Ramones was highly unusual in that he played four beats on the hi-hat for every one on the snare drum, which is very difficult to do at fast speeds. If it was good enough for The Ramones, it was good enough for me. I chose to play it the hard way.

Saturday night, we played our ten original songs, and then to round out the set, we added covers such as "Orgasm Addict" by the Buzzcocks, "I Think We're Alone Now" by Tommy James and The Shondells, "Garage Band" and "Janie Jones" by The Clash, "Seventeen" by The Sex Pistols and "Do You Wanna Dance" and "Blitzkrieg Bop" by The Ramones. For encores, we repeated some of the same songs we had already played. The show probably lasted only 45 minutes because our adrenaline caused us to play the songs at a much faster speed than we had practiced them at.

The Meteoric Rise of The Reactions

Which begs the obvious confession: the drummer is the one responsible for playing the songs at the correct speed. It is not considered a compliment to say that the songs were played at a much faster speed than rehearsed at. But it sounded **really good** at those blazing speeds. So accidently, that became our trademark sound.

My hands and feet were playing faster than I had ever dreamed of. It felt as if I was having an out-of-body experience, like I was watching myself play. When my eyes finally focused, I noticed that Chris Cottie, the drummer of The Eat, was only a few feet away at the side of the dance floor, staring at me while I played the drums. The Eat was already one of the great bands in South Florida. Although they never made it out of Florida, they remain one of my all-time favorite punk bands. *Miami New Times*, which is the closest thing South Florida has to *The Village Voice*, ranks them as the #2 punk band of all time. They have one of the few records that are more expensive than Reactions vinyl. Chris Cottie was a beast of a drummer. Literally. A big, hairy, mountain size man that hit the drums with an unseen-before ferociousness. He was also very skilled, very precise, and very creative. I was a skinny 17-year-old that hadn't even started shaving yet, playing to a paying public for only the second time in my life. Very humbling.

After the show, Chris Cottie told me that he had never seen a drummer play as fast as me. He didn't think it was possible to play every stroke the way I did at the speeds we were playing. I wanted to tell him that I didn't think it was possible either, but I probably just grunted, and said "Thank you."

That night, The Reactions instantaneously took the throne as South Florida's top "New Wave" band. When The Agora

The Meteoric Rise of The Reactions

Ballroom began hosting New Wave Tuesdays, The Reactions were the perennial headliner. We were also the de-facto opening band for any visiting groups that remotely resembled punk rock.

In January 1980, The Agora Ballroom, one of the most revered rock institutions in America, opened in Hallandale. Isaac and I went to the very first concert: Rick Derringer. We had loved it when Rick Derringer played "Hang On Sloopy," but that represented the past. New Wave Tuesdays was the present, and the future, and it was really exciting to be a part of. While The Agora Ballroom was in its glory we got to see great bands such as U2, Iggy Pop, The Kinks, Sly and The Family Stone, Lords of The New Church, Muddy Waters, and so many others.

The first huge gig for The Reactions was at The Agora, opening for The Ramones in front of a packed house. The next eight years would have me cross paths many times with the great Joey Ramone. The most random and unlikely was an encounter a few years later in Hialeah, Florida. The Ramones were playing a full-fledged concert at Sunrise Arena, 25 miles away in Ft. Lauderdale. After his concert, guess who showed up at the bar in Hialeah that I was playing at with my band at the time, The Spinouts. Fucking Joey Ramone! The singer of The Spinouts, Steve Lambert, and I were outside getting some air after we had played our set, and Joey Ramone just showed up out of thin air. Who would have ever imagined that Joey Ramone would take a 30-minute cab drive after his own concert in Ft. Lauderdale to go see local bands play? In Hialeah of all places. We were speechless. One of the cover songs that our band regularly played was "Needles and Pins." The Ramones had just released "Needles and Pins" on their most recent Phil Spector produced album. We asked Joey if he would play it with us after The Front, the other band playing that night, finished their set, and he said yes. Still to this day, Joey Ramone singing "Needles and

The Meteoric Rise of The Reactions

Pins" with us at a Big Daddy's in Hialeah ranks as one of the great highlights of my life. I literally had goose bumps as we were playing it.

Many years later in New York City, Joey Ramone took a personal interest in the progress of Circus of Power, a band that I helped form. The Ramone's world-famous producer, Daniel Rey, ended up producing two fabulous albums for Circus of Power. Joey Ramone was the embodiment of perseverance… a trailblazing pioneer who became one of the greatest music legends of all time. I feel honored to have hung out with him.

Gabba-gabba-hey in peace Joey Ramone.

The next step for The Reactions was to get signed to a record label. Considering how fast everything was progressing, it seemed that within short order we would be signed to a major record label, record an album, and embark on a national concert tour. This would of course rapidly lead to the fame and success that we all thought was inevitable. If only it happened this way.

In the meanwhile, The Reactions continued to headline The Agora, garnering remarkable accolades from the press, while Isaac and I enjoyed newfound attention from girls. Tony, who did not possess what we universally consider as traditional good looks, scored himself a gorgeous, Porsche-driving girlfriend named Maggie, who was completely out of his league. Tony was an intelligent man. He ended up marrying Maggie.

Before I had yet even dropped out of high school, I found myself in situations that I had to pinch myself to believe were real. One night at The Agora, a pretty, I dare say wholesome-looking girl, started making small talk with me by the backstage entrance. We were scheduled to go on stage in about a half hour, so I just came

The Meteoric Rise of The Reactions

right out and asked her if she would give me a blowjob before I played.

"Are you serious?" she asked with an incredulous look on her face.

I looked her right in the eyes, and without smiling told her that I was indeed, serious.

Of course, I thought she was gonna slap me, or at least walk away, but instead said, "Okay, where?"

Wearing the same Beach High Hi-Tides baseball jacket that I had worn earlier that day to school, we went to her car in the parking lot and she started to give me a blowjob. My eyes were beginning to well up with tears of joy, till I heard a sharp rap on the window. It was a Hallandale police officer with a big steel flashlight pointed inside of the car, motioning for us to get out. He checked our IDs and his head almost ignited when it clicked that I was a 17-year-old boy getting a blowjob in the parking lot of a bar from a 22-year-old girl. After a stern lecture, he ordered me to get the hell away from the club and let the girl go free. I doubled-back to the bar and played a one-and-a-half-hour show that night, but never saw the wholesome blowjob girl again.

Believe me, I looked for her!

My recently acquired fame changed things at school also. Popular girls that would have previously been insulted had I dared even say hi to them in the halls were coming up to me and gushing, "Hi Joey!" I harbored too much past resentment to fall for the new attention I was now receiving. However, I did consent when the most beautiful girl in all of Beach High (I won't say her name here…okay shhh, don't tell anyone, but it

The Meteoric Rise of The Reactions

was Pam F.) allowed me to come over to her house on Pine Tree Drive when her parents weren't home. This is a girl that I normally would have had a less than zero shot with. A month later, I dumped her! This was success at the local level. Can you imagine what fame on a national level would be like?

The guys in The Reactions were all hungry to succeed. We knew that regardless of how well things were going locally, we needed to get out of Florida to really make it. So that became our goal. All of us, except Johnny, had the luxury of being young enough to dedicate ourselves exclusively to The Reactions without having to worry about any repercussions should we fail. Isaac and I were 18 and 17 years old respectively, and if we wasted another year or two with the band, would still have plenty of time to pursue something else. Tony's family had a thriving business that would still be available for him, if need be.

Johnny's only hope was music. He had bounced around in the state juvenile system, and wasn't likely to ever go back to school, or frankly, to ever hold down any sort of a mainstream job. If The Reactions failed, Johnny would have to do this all over again with another band. Mind you, neither of us ever even conceived of the possibility of failing, but other than me dropping out of high school, the cost so far had been minimal. At this point, success had come quickly and easily, and nobody had been forced to make any difficult "life" decisions yet.

The next logical step was to record a demo of our songs so that we could shop it to record labels. With $1,000 given to us by Tony's dad, we booked eight hours in a 24-track recording studio. We were young, and none of us had ever stepped foot inside of a recording studio before. Although we sounded good when we played live shows, where sloppy playing can be categorized as "rock and roll," recording those same songs in a

The Meteoric Rise of The Reactions

professional recording studio was altogether different and required a much higher level of technical musical expertise. We were all acceptably good musicians, but not yet nearly as good as experienced studio musicians. Remember, it takes a long time to get really great on a musical instrument. Most groups that are discovered "overnight" have probably been together as a band for five to ten years, and are closer to 30 years of age, rather than to 20. We weren't even 20 yet. To compensate for our lack of studio experience, we decided to play the songs as simply as possible and to let the quality of the songs and the heart that we put into it shine through.

A big mistake we made as a result of our inexperience was that instead of recording four songs and getting them to sound really great, we recorded ten songs. It is impossible to record and properly produce ten songs in only one 8-hour studio session. Heck, getting one song to sound great can take a full day, or even much longer. Another mistake we made was....well, we were astoundingly high during the entire recording session. Johnny had brought along some killer Thai Stick. Everything sounds great when you're high, but afterwards when you come down, you wonder, "What the fuck was that!" For providing us with a demo, thankfully, it turned out good enough.

Our First Record

Now that we had our songs recorded, what were we supposed to do with them? It's hard enough if you live in New York City or Los Angeles to get your demo listened to by someone in any kind of a position to do anything about it. In 1980 South Florida, there wasn't a single person whose job it was to discover the next potential breakout music artist. We never expected success to be easy, and we were willing to fight for it, but the sheer magnitude of the uphill struggle was astounding. How many local bands do you know that are written about by the press as the second coming of The Beatles and sign autographs at their gigs. None! I recently ran into a successful 35-year-old punk rock musician who was signed to a major record label, and he was stoked to meet the drummer of Battalion of Saints (me). When he put two and two together and realized that I was the drummer of The Reactions as well, he **really** flipped out. He told me he had a friend who would just shit when he told him that he had met me in person. This is 30 years after the fact, and as insane as it all sounds, that's how passionate people have always been regarding The Reactions. It should not have been so overwhelmingly difficult for a band, seemingly as special as ours, to get some kind of a break.

Our expectation was that somehow a record label A&R person would hear about the success of the band and would either set up a showcase performance or get our demo tape listened to by a record executive. A&R, which stands for artist and repertoire, are the scouts that find acts to join the talent stables of the record companies that they work for. Nothing along those lines

Our First Record

materialized quick enough for our hyper expectations. If a record company was not going to help us produce and sell our records, then we would have to do it ourselves.

Neither Isaac nor I had any experience at all with any aspect of producing a record, but as the saying goes, where there's a will there's a way, so Isaac and I just took it step by step. As can be expected, we made a few mistakes along the way. The finished product was a bare bone, minimally produced, dirt-cheap record, which was funded by $1,500 that was advanced to us from a friend of ours named Errol "Spike" Walzer, who had recently inherited some money after his father passed away.

We took our studio recording tape to Criteria Studios in North Miami so they could cut a master disc from it. Criteria is a world-class facility and is well known for recording some of Eric Clapton's best works. When the master disc was ready a few days later, we drove it directly to Miami Tape, Inc., in the warehouse district of Hialeah. Miami Tape was a reputable vinyl record company, and they did a lot of work for local heroes, KC and the Sunshine Band, who happened to live close by in Miami Lakes. Miami Tape did high quality work and charged only $1 per record. From the master disc that Criteria had made for us, Miami Tape produced a mother disk to stamp the 500 records that we ordered.

To produce the artwork, we hired Miami Tape again. Errol came up with a simple, yet striking design that featured a black and white picture of the band with a red border around it and THE REACTIONS written in sloping letters at the very top. OFFICIAL RELEASE, the name of the record, was written in red on the top left corner of our picture. The record cover opened like a book to reveal a collage made up of the numerous pictures

Our First Record

that Errol himself had snapped during the previous, fast-paced six months. It was a simple record cover, but it did the trick.

The four songs that we chose for the record, as already described, were recorded with very little sophistication. With only $2,500 to spend on the entire project, a talented producer was not in our budget. A great producer knows how to take a good band and record them so that they sound like a great band, and take a great band, and turn them into superstars. The closest we came to a producer was the engineer that was included in the price of the studio, and as helpful as he was to our young band, it just wasn't the same as having a producer who is financially vested in the success of the body of work he is producing. For now, it was all about releasing our songs; "Tonight," "In Society," "It's Our Turn Now," and especially, "Marianne," the sure-fire hit that would make us rich and famous.

While we were waiting for the vinyl and artwork to be ready, we entered into the South Florida Rising Stars contest at The Agora. The contest was divided into three separate nights of competitions in three different categories: Punk, Pop Rock, and Hard Rock. All of the music had to be original. The victors in each of the three categories would then face-off in the finals.

The Reactions competed in the Punk category. At stake was not only the opportunity to be included in the finals, but also, the winner's entire 30-minute set would be played the following Friday night on the local mega FM radio station, WSHE. On the very first song, Isaac broke not one, but two guitar strings! He did not have a backup guitar, so he did the best he could by playing with just four strings. It sounded hideous! I thought for sure that we had no chance of winning, but the strength of the bass and drums, Tony's singing, and the originality of the songs pulled us through. By some miracle, the judges declared us the

Our First Record

winners and we moved on to the finals. When they played our entire set on the radio so tens of thousands of potential new fans could finally hear the great Reactions, I cringed. It was awful.

The finals were held on September 18th, 1980 and pitted Freewheel, The Kids, and The Reactions against each other. This was the best of the best of South Florida rock and roll. We played very well and most people in the audience thought that either The Reactions or The Kids should have won. Disappointingly, the judges announced Freewheel as the winner with The Reactions coming in second. All of the members of Freewheel were really good, polished musicians, but their performance that night was unremarkable.

The Kids on the other hand, were fabulous! They played a refreshing set of upbeat, original pop songs and sang with multi-layers of harmonious vocals. The Kids were all truly excellent musicians and of course, Johnny Depp soon-after joined the band on guitar. We were good friends with The Kids and often hung out together. I wish that I had some crazy and entertaining, "This one time with Johnny Depp…" stories, but Johnny and I were both barely 17 years old when we started playing at The Agora. The truth is that we both were pretty quiet and usually went along with what everybody else was doing, and 17 or not, neither of us ever passed on the chance to enjoy cocktails at the bar, or since we were always low on funds, more often in the parking lot as well. I will admit that once, as I was looking up at Johnny playing his guitar up on stage, I said aloud to Isaac, "Man, that kid is really good-looking." Regardless of his mysterious persona, Johnny has never forgotten where he came from and has never spared any effort or expense to help his friends. He remains a humble guy true to his rock and roll roots, and we are all insanely proud of him, as he was one of us.

Our First Record

In 2008, the bass player of The Kids, the supremely talented Bruce Witkin, organized a two-night benefit concert in Pompano Beach, Florida, in honor of his recently deceased mother, Sheila Witkin, who for many years promoted original music in the South Florida area. Sheila Witkin, during a very dark time for rock and roll, when disco was all the rage, fought fiercely to get the original bands that she represented, booked and paid at clubs. She had a profound effect on Isaac Baruch and I, who as underage teenagers, were regulars at the Tight Squeeze club that she managed. We would watch the band Tight Squeeze play and dream that one day we would be as good as they were. Through her contacts, she helped Coz Canler, one of the band members of Tight Squeeze, join The Romantics. All of the bands playing at the memorial concert had some kind of connection with the South Florida music scene and to Sheila Witkin. The Reactions were invited to open for The Kids on the second night of the benefit. Isaac and I were unable to locate the original singer of The Reactions, Tony Suppa, so we had Alex Mitchel, the singer of Circus of Power, fly in from Los Angeles to replace him. Unfortunately, Johnny Salton's health was badly deteriorating at the time, so Ricky Mahler, also from Circus of Power, replaced him. Johnny Salton, who passed away only a few months after the concert, had an almost cult-like following in South Florida. Just as many people felt that because of his nasty drug habits, he had wasted his talents. But there is something very final about death that demands that things be put into the proper perspective. It now didn't matter if Johnny was a genius or a fuck up. He was dead. He was gone forever. His funeral marked an incredibly sad day for me, and an important part of my past died with him.

Because of Johnny Depp's participation in the concert, it was a huge event. I was worried that the crowd would be mostly young girls screaming for Johnny, and who would ignore

Our First Record

everything else. Turned out that Johnny did have a nice contingent of screaming girls camped in front of him, but the majority of the audience was very appreciative and very enthusiastic towards the whole event. We are all much better musicians now, and it showed when we played our set. It was an exciting and memorable night for all the musicians and fans that were there to celebrate one of the most exciting eras of original music in South Florida. Thank you Bruce and thank you Johnny!

Within a month of winning our category in the battle of the bands, our records and covers were finally ready. It may not seem like much, but it meant a lot to see our picture on a record cover, and in a way, the record validated the band. As the great French philosopher Descartes might have said had he been a musician, "We have a record, therefore we are a band."

Or something like that.

We needed this…we needed to see some tangible progress.

Ours was a true DIY project, and what followed next can't possibly be spun to seem glamorous. We had to fold and glue all of the 500 covers by hand, stuff them with records, and then slip a plastic protective outer sleeve over each one. The entire band pitched in and we spent two long days in Isaac's bedroom knocking out the tedious job.

To distribute the records, Isaac and I literally drove to each of the local record stores and asked the store owners and managers to display our record. Fortunately, all of the local record stores were happy to oblige. Vibrations, Peaches, Blue Note Records, Specs Music, Yesterday and Today Records, and the biggest supporters of local, alternative music, Ted Gottfried and Leslie Wimmer at Open Books and Records, all prominently displayed

Our First Record

our new record. Every week or two, we would drive back to each of the stores to collect the money owed us and to replenish the records that had been sold. Errol was supposed to receive the money that we collected, but not much ever made it back to him. Whatever money was collected just went back into our pockets, ….I mean, into the band of course. Errol eventually figured out that he was never going to recoup his investment, but he didn't seem concerned, or even overly surprised by that revelation. Errol believed in The Reactions and was happy to help in any way that he could.

The band sorely lacked any type of professional management. A friend of the band, Richard Schindler, booked our shows and held the title of band manager, but he was not a true, sophisticated, well-connected band manager. For the most part, it was Isaac and I that did most of the legwork and conjured up the marketing ideas. By printing clever flyers and placing them on car windows at clubs, we anticipated that our records would magically sell out and that a second pressing would be required. We were a bit naive and over-optimistic, as only about 175 copies sold during the first four months after the record's release. Instead of getting discouraged, we doubled down our effort by contacting two large independent record distributors, Rough Trade and Gem Records, that we had read about in the popular national punk fanzines, *Flipside* and *Maximum Rocknroll*. Isaac and I cold-called both companies, and after giving our record a listen, each agreed to purchase and distribute 50 records. After such a tepid start locally, we felt vindicated when prestigious national and international distributors, despite never having heard of us, decided to get involved with our record.

But without the support of a sharp management team, we had no idea how to build upon that progress. The jump from struggling to sell 500 records at $5 a pop, to blowing out 50,000

Our First Record

records, can be remarkably quick; it could be just one or two breaks away. A magazine article, an influential radio DJ, a mention on TV, or a big shot producer might have been all that we needed for that big break. But since we hadn't yet figured out how to make the jump nationally, we remained just a local band, albeit one with a powder keg of potential. Our popularity was still growing, but since it wasn't growing at the same hyperbolic rate as nine months ago, it felt like a slowdown to us. We were playing to enthusiastic audiences at The Agora and anywhere else punk rock was welcomed, but the underlying feeling by the public, and certainly by us, was that more was to be expected.

More was expected **for** us, and more was expected **from** us.

Florida is quicksand for anything creative or out of the ordinary. We might not have been sinking, yet, but we were stuck in the mud. We had to do something to get the fuck out of Florida.

A Jamaican Record Label to the Rescue…Yah Mon!

By the end of 1980, a lot of popular bands like The Police, Joe Jackson, and The Clash were getting major airplay with their great, reggae inspired rock songs. The combination of reggae and rock sounded fantastic, and many of those songs became big hits. "Roxanne" by The Police, "The Harder They Come" by Joe Jackson, and many songs by The Clash, including "Pressure Drop" were played as reggae songs, but had the rawness and balls of a rock song. It was a brilliant combination of musical styles and The Reactions wanted in. We were definitely at a point where we needed to try and shake things up a bit, so Isaac Baruch and Tony Suppa, two of the most prolific song writers most people have never heard of, started cranking out reggae and ska influenced rock songs. Reggae, and ska, which is more upbeat than reggae, are Jamaican inspired styles of music that rely on subtlety. Our renditions were not very subtle, but they sounded good, and so became a part of our sets. Yah Mon!

As I previously mentioned, there weren't any record company representatives in South Florida…unless you sang in Spanish or played "Island Music." That normally would not have been an option, but given this newfound addition to our music arsenal, a well-respected Jamaican record label, Ranking Records, began to show an interest in us. I'm not sure if it was the novelty of white punk rockers playing reggae and ska, or if they wanted to sign the next Clash, but it didn't matter to us. A record label was interested in us. Ranking Records definitely had the firepower to get us out of Florida, and if they were interested in us, then we were interested in them.

A Jamaican Record Label to the Rescue...Yah Mon!

After a few months of courting us they arranged for a showcase concert at Fire and Ice, a large, fancy club in the design district of Miami. We were accustomed to playing mostly in dingy rock and roll bars, and even though the Miami design district was nothing like the super ritzy area it is now, this cavernous nightclub was very upscale. The executives from Ranking Records were flying in from Kingston, Jamaica for the sole purpose of evaluating us to determine if we would be offered a record contract or not.

The night of our showcase concert, fate surly stepped in to alter our collective futures.

I developed an intense pain in my stomach at around 9 p.m. It came on suddenly and unexpectedly. We were due to play at around 11 p.m., so I was confident that I could tough it out for a few hours. As far as I was concerned, this was the most important night of my life. All of us were almost singularly focused on getting signed to a record label. It would have been the crowning achievement of our young, driven lives. I drank ginger ale and set aside the pain. An hour and a half later, with tears in my eyes, I told Isaac that I couldn't take it anymore, and that I needed to go to the hospital. The tears were from the disappointment that I was letting everybody down, not from the pain in my stomach, which was now almost unbearable. My girlfriend drove me to the hospital where I was immediately put on a morphine drip.

When I woke up the next morning, all three of my bandmates were at my bedside. I immediately started to apologize but stopped when I saw that Isaac had a wry grin on his face.

A Jamaican Record Label to the Rescue...Yah Mon!

"Why are you smiling?" I asked. The only thing I could think about was that I had singlehandedly ruined our chances of a record deal.

"Tony never made it to the club last night. He got lost and couldn't find it. He never showed up," Isaac said with his smile fading only slightly.

"What? How is that possible?" I asked.

"Doesn't matter. Fuck it. It's not meant to be," he consoled me. "Just worry about getting better."

It had been **only** the most important night of our lives. But just like that, Isaac dismissed it as if it were nothing. Fate had intervened, and there wasn't anything that anybody could have done about it. Instead of focusing on what a major fuck up this was, and the many what ifs that could have been, Isaac instantly knew that would not have done anybody any good. We were already a close-knit band. That night, we cemented our relationship. Our bond and our commitment to each other ascended to a new level. We were more resolved than ever to collect on the success that we were due.

The Reactions were not a band to rest on laurels. We were perfectionists. We often rehearsed the day of a gig if we thought we weren't playing well enough yet. Most rock bands are too cool, or too lazy, to rehearse the day of a show. Supposedly, it takes away from the spontaneity and energy of that night's performance. We were at the very top of the local music food chain, and yet we still wanted to improve, so we rehearsed incessantly.

A Jamaican Record Label to the Rescue...Yah Mon!

The entire time, Isaac and Tony had been constantly writing new songs. Every few weeks or so, there was a new song to learn, arrange, and polish. These were all very good, useable songs. Within a year, we had 25 strong original songs on our play list. We basically had two complete albums of material ready to go, but no record label. We would have loved a little help or a little guidance, but after the Ranking Records fiasco, we weren't going to sit around waiting for it. We decided to take matters into our own hands and make another record. And this time, it was a great record.

That's No Way to Spend Your Youth

By 1981, The Reactions had improved significantly from the pure rawness of the Blue Waters era. We were still quite raw, but our songs were now a bit more complex and contained an added subtlety that we previously had lacked. Isaac and Tony's song writing had evolved, but they were still writing great pop songs with gigantic hooks. We would take those sweet, upbeat songs into the practice room, which was still Isaac's mother's guest room, and turn them into "Reactions" songs. The four of us were usually tuned in to the same idea of what the finished song should sound like. If anybody had any thoughts about the way a song should be played, we tried it, and it was usually pretty easy to decide if it worked, or if it didn't work. Within an hour or two, the song was usually a finished product.

We were a little older now. I was 18, Isaac was 19, Tony was 20, and Johnny was 24, and were starting to enjoy a little more "rock star" swagger. We didn't have a full-time professional manager capable of getting us the national attention that we craved and deserved, so Isaac and I should have probably focused more on the business end of the band. Instead, we took advantage of the band's popularity to party our asses off. I'm just being honest!

The Reactions had appeared in South Florida just as the punk movement was getting started. The scene was small, and it was usually the same 100 or so people that attended each of the shows. What brought us all together was a common dislike of the stale, boring music that dominated the radio airwaves; the Journey, Styx, and Rush types of bands. We were also tired of

That's No Way to Spend Your Youth

the narrow-minded people that went hand-in-hand with those dinosaur bands. We were sick of it, and needed Elvis Costello, The Clash, and Sex Pistols types of bands to save us. Locally, that meant going to see The Eat, The Cichlids, The Kids, Critical Mass, and Charlie Picket and the Eggs, who along with many other exciting local bands, including The Reactions of course, contributed to making the era, hands down, the golden age of South Florida original music. Isaac and I thoroughly enjoyed hanging out with so many like-minded, fun people, and we did our best to keep ourselves under control, which wasn't always easy. On what seemed like a regular basis, as the evening and his buzz would progress, inevitably, Isaac would expose his dick. Eventually, that became his "thing" and crowds of people would egg him on to whip it out. You'd hear yelled from across the club, "Isaac, let's see your dick!" It almost got us banned from our beloved Agora Ballroom when Isaac took it out on stage.

Isaac and I were just hanging out and drinking at the bar in The Agora, when at about 11 p.m. we each popped a Quaalude. At around 11:30 when The Screaming Sneakers were getting ready to play "Do You Love Me" by the Dave Clark Five, the strong effects of the Quaaludes began to kick in. For that song, Randy Blitz, their very accomplished, flamboyant drummer would leave his drum kit to sing the song and another band member, normally the guitar player, Eddie Gregg, or the singer, Lisa Nash, would man the drums. Neither of us was expecting to hear, "Will Isaac Baruch and Joey Wrecked of The Reactions please join us on stage?" Trust me, Quaaludes rarely encourage one to make the right decision, and this was no exception. We joined them onstage. Isaac had a good old time jamming his guitar and bouncing around on the stage, and I got more than one dirty look from Randy Blitz for my sloppy drumming. At the end of the song, Isaac tore to the front of the stage, pushed aside his guitar, and you guessed it...exposed his dick!

That's No Way to Spend Your Youth

Management at The Agora wanted to ban us, as they had banned The Eat just because the O'Brien brothers, Eddie and John, had cursed and spit on the stage. We vehemently denied that Isaac had actually taken it out (he definitely did), and eventually, they just let us off with a stern warning.

At one point, both Isaac and I had steady girlfriends. Both of them were free-spirited and very social-minded, so hanging out with our girlfriends did nothing to slow the party down. I'd venture to say they even added fuel to the fire. Isaac's girlfriend was Pam Axley from the eclectic, all-girl noise band, Sheer Smegma. She looked like the waspy, upper-class daughter of an old-money Palm Beach family, but she was dirty, dirty, dirty! What a woman. She was perfect for Isaac. Sheer Smegma recorded a record in Isaac's bedroom using a four-track reel-to-reel recorder that Isaac mixed with the help of our sound tech guru friend, David Camp. The record was later re-released by the dynamic Jello Biafra (Dead Kennedys) on his California based Alternative Tentacle Records label on 12-inch vinyl as Teddy and The Frat Girls. Guess who the drummer on the record, Josephine Dupont, really is? I had to do something with my time and talent, didn't I?

My girlfriend was also perfect for me. She was 18 years of age and looked like a sophisticated NYC magazine model. She had an angular haircut of chestnut brown hair that covered half of her face. I had never seen anything like her. She was 5' 2" and weighed only about 105 lbs., so she certainly wasn't a NYC magazine model, but she was very metropolitan, and did model for local department store catalogues. She dressed cool, and not at all like most other girls in South Florida. She also knew more about good, relatively obscure bands than I did. Sonnie Daze, who would quickly become my girlfriend, walked up to me one night The Reactions were playing at The Balkan Rock Club in

That's No Way to Spend Your Youth

Dania Beach and asked me if I wanted to do a line of really good blow. Those were the first words she ever said to me. I was intrigued that she emphasized "really good" as if just offering me some coke wasn't enough. Heck, now I had to try it. I wasn't a big fan of cocaine, but she was really cute, so I took her backstage and did a line with her. It really was good coke! She then disappeared. Just when I gave up on ever seeing her again, she appeared after the show was over as we were putting the equipment away. I asked her if she had a friend for Isaac so we could all go and get a drink together. That's when I first made the acquaintance of Rose Ortiz, Sonnie's best friend. Sonnie and Rose would become pivotal players during my seven-year musical odyssey. After the equipment was all loaded into Isaac's Toyota hatchback station wagon, the four of us, me driving Sonnie's black Mazda RX-7 and Isaac driving his Toyota station wagon, stopped at Johnny's Liquors on Federal Highway in Hallandale and bought a bottle of Southern Comfort to take to the beach with us. On the way to the beach, we stopped at our friend Paul's house to buy pharmaceutical Quaaludes. At first, Paul was livid that we had awakened him at 3 a.m., but after he saw that we were with two girls, was nice enough to sell us the ludes at such an inconvenient hour. It was during nights like this that I was grateful for being a rock musician. I couldn't imagine any of my friends who were attending college being around the interesting, artistic people that I was around and doing the unique, adventurous things that I was doing. What I did not pay much heed to was how dangerous those adventures sometimes were. We drank at the bar and snorted a line of blow at the gig. Afterwards, we washed down our Quaaludes with a bottle of Southern Comfort. Finally, at 7 a.m., we all checked into a $21 hotel room at the Paradise Inn on 85th Street and Harding Ave. on Miami Beach. The story could have obviously had a very different ending.

That's No Way to Spend Your Youth

But we were fine, so the next day just before noon, we walked across the street to take a dip in the beautiful Atlantic Ocean. It was a gorgeous, bright, sunny day with a light breeze that considerably lessened the humidity. The warm, calm water was a totally see-through shade of light green, and the fine sand underneath our feet was smooth and soft. It was a beautiful morning to be at the beach, even if it was just for a short while. Johnny and Denise met us there, and we felt like rock stars; like Mick Jagger, Keith Richards, and Ronnie Wood of The Rolling Stones, hanging out at the beach as everybody wondered who the hell these freaks were. After breakfast at Denny's on 69th Street and Collins Avenue, Isaac and I bid a fond farewell to Sonnie and Rose, and the three band members took the short drive back to Isaac's to meet up with Tony Suppa and Richard Schindler. It was time to discuss the band's future, and the making of our second record.

The meeting at Isaac's house lasted less than an hour. We all knew what had to happen. We needed to record and press a fabulous record, get signed to a major record label, and get out of Florida. Despite the extreme odds that were still against us, to a man, we were absolutely convinced that it would work out exactly as planned.

Isaac, Tony, and I had already previously discussed taking the band to NYC where we were much more likely to be noticed and signed to a record label but had ruled it out because we didn't think Johnny was capable of surviving without Denise, who was now fully supporting him financially. Denise was not willing to leave South Florida just to support Johnny. The three of us would have been fine gutting it out in NYC, as we all had no issue with finding jobs to pay our way, but none of us even considered the idea of supporting Johnny. We therefore ruled out leaving town without the support of a record label. The burden of having to carry Johnny became the first major obstacle that The Reactions had to face. This was a biggie. I was no longer a 17-year-old high school kid. As satisfactory as my music career was progressing, I realized that as good as we were, possibly because of Johnny, it might not work out. Tony was also starting to be pressured by his father to join "the family business." I can't say for certain if it was true what the press was saying about Tony's father being involved in the upper echelons of organized crime, because I don't know exactly what type of business Tony's family was in. But I do know that Tony was needed to help run it. So, we'll just leave it at that. Isaac, who had an obvious gift for writing great songs, was committed to staying in the music business, but also shared the frustration of being stuck in South Florida because of Johnny. In spite of facing our first real head winds, we were still confident that a major label would sign us, and the Johnny problem would be solved.

The first order of business at our band meeting was to figure out where to get the money to pay for time at a recording studio. Richard Schindler came up with the great idea to sell beer at The Coconut Grove Art Festival that was coming up in a few weeks. Richard was not a great band manager, at least not for the purpose that we needed a band manager for. He was however, an excellent businessperson and knew how to make money. He devised a plan for us to buy 50 cases of beer from a local distributor in a not-so-nice part of Miami on 79th Street and Biscayne Blvd., for 25 cents a can. On the first day of the two-day art show, we stuffed the beers into big garbage bags filled with ice to keep them cold and set up camp at the edge of the festival in Richard's van and in Isaac's Toyota station wagon. We then moved the beer into Styrofoam coolers, walked into the festival and sold the ice-cold beer for $1 a can. Nowadays, beer is sold all over the festival and is more expensive. In 1981, they were not yet selling beer at the art festival. At least we didn't think they were, so the entire market was ours. The cops, if they saw us, would ask us to stop. But five minutes later, we sold beers again. Even the cops realized we were providing a much-needed service. In the hot sun we were able to sell beer literally as fast as it took to get it into the festival. Before the end of the second day, we had sold all 50 cases of beer, netting out a profit of just under $1,000. We now had the money to record our new record.

The Reactions Love You

Isaac rang up Tony Mancino at Music Recording Labs in Ft. Lauderdale and booked five hours of studio time at $85 per hour. Tony Mancino, and his partner Barry Seiver, owned the first-class, cutting-edge studio and had done a superb job of recording The Cichlids there. The Cichlids had a massive local following and were the most popular original music band in South Florida before The Reactions hit the scene. Debbie DeNeese, the talented, energetic singer, Susan Robins, the sexy, scowling bass player, Bobby Tak, the hyper-aggressive drummer, and guitarist Allan Portman, might have been a little bubble gummy for many hardcore punk fans, but I loved them. *Be True To Your School*, the album they recorded with Mancino, should have been a national success. Unfortunately, they also went the way of most of the South Florida bands of the era, meaning they died an untimely, early death.

On Saturday, March 14th, 1981, The Reactions were set to record their second record. With only $1,000 to spend on this recording, we were on a really tight budget. For two solid weeks we met every day at Isaac's house to practice only the six or seven songs that we were considering recording, so we could get them super tight. We finally decided to record just four new songs: "Nights on End," "Rebel Rousers," "I Can't Help It," and "Be My Girl." All four had the potential to be big hits. They were pop songs that if you weren't singing along to after hearing them only twice, it meant you were just dead inside. They were that good. We also decided to re-record our best song, "Marianne" because we didn't like the way it had turned out on the first record.

The Reactions Love You

Saturday finally came, and we were scheduled to record at 8 p.m. sharp. We were excited, and we were ready, but trust me when I tell you that not a single member of The Reactions was at Music Recording Labs at 8 p.m. that Saturday.

How can I explain how it was possible that nobody made it there on time and ready to record? Five hours in the studio was already not enough time to set up and mike our instruments, balance the sound levels, record the rhythm tracks, rhythm guitars, lead guitars, lead vocals, and background vocals and then reduce all of those tracks into the two stereo tracks that the vinyl record would then be mastered from. Tony Mancino, who was engineering the session, needed as much time as possible to mix all of those tracks into a polished recording that captured the true sound, the essence if you will, of The Reactions. Most likely, this was our last chance. Our budget only allowed for the project to be completed in five short hours, so it had to be done expeditiously. We all knew this. So how was it possible that nobody arrived on time?

I had planned to get to Isaac's house in Surfside at 7 p.m., which would give us time to load the drums, guitars, and amps into the Toyota station wagon, and still make it to the studio on time. At the last moment, Sonnie called and asked if she could come watch us record. I thought it would be cool to have her there, so I agreed to pick her up at her mom's house in Miami Lakes, which was in the opposite direction of the recording studio. Isaac seemed okay with it, but probably because I wasn't completely forthright with him as to how far out of the way she lived. So at around 7:35, off we went from Isaac's house to pick her up. We were already running late. I had never been to Sonnie's house in Miami Lakes, which is configured like a giant maze. She had given me instructions to get there, but after 20 minutes of twists and turns, we still had no idea where her house was, so we had to double back to the convenience store by the interstate to call her from a pay phone. The good news was that she lived only five minutes away and the bad news was that it was now already 8:30, and Ft. Lauderdale was still far away. The two of us remained pretty cool about the situation and even went inside the convenience store to buy a six-pack of beer for the ride. We picked up Sonnie, cracked open some beers, and started heading toward the studio. At around 9:20 we finally got to the studio. I felt horribly guilty. The primary reason that Isaac and I were late was because I wanted to impress my brand-new girlfriend. My guilt quickly turned to anger when Tony Mancino informed us that Tony and Johnny had already been there but had left to find a music store that was open so that Johnny could buy new bass strings. We had asked Johnny to replace his old bass strings two weeks ago, but he obviously hadn't done so. Tonight, when he arrived at the studio and began to warm up, he noticed that the bass sound, not surprisingly, was dull, so Tony Suppa volunteered to drive him to a music store. It wasn't till after 10 p.m. that they finally returned, and they hadn't even found a music store that was open, so Johnny was going to have to record with old, dull bass strings!

By starting so late, we had squandered over two hours of a five hour $85 per hour recording session. It may not sound like a big deal, but this was 1980, and $85 an hour was a fortune. To put it into perspective, buying $3.50 drumsticks, $6.00 guitar strings, and $15.00 bass strings was a big deal to us. The extra $170 may just as well have been $1,700. We just didn't have it. But there's a unique quality that most artistic types share. We generally don't get too caught up or too uptight about rigid rules or about circumstances beyond our control. We were there to create, and there is never a forced timetable for the creative process to play out. It would have been impossible to play our instruments freely had we been thinking about whether we were late or how much time we had, or whether the bass might sound a little dull. The instant we started playing, the magic of our musical chemistry quickly overcame any lingering negative thoughts. I could immediately tell it was going to be a special night. Fortunately, Tony Mancino was into it as much as we were and was not going to let our tardiness and lack of money get in the way of doing a top-notch job for us.

We had come into the studio very well prepared. We played "I Can't Help It" to warm up and so that Mancino could balance the sound levels. After that, we were ready to roll the tape. Johnny and I layed down the bass and drum tracks of all five songs in only one or two takes each. It was obvious from the get-go that we were grooving well together, which made it easier for Isaac to add in the rhythm guitar parts right afterwards. We were playing with as much control and precision as we were capable of, but our youthful energy was still apparent. Tony Suppa followed next in the vocals booth and knocked out the lead vocals just as effortlessly. Finally, like two cherries being added on the top of an ice cream sundae, the background vocals and lead guitars topped off the recording session. I believe that by around 12:30 a.m., all of the tracks were on tape. Although it had sounded very good, if not close to perfect on the playbacks, it would have been easy to miss something. We now had to wait, hope, and stress that we hadn't botched anything that might render any of the tracks un-useable.

Tony Mancino immediately began to mix each of the 16 tracks, one by one. For the first song, he isolated each of our instruments to get our individual feedback. I told him that I wanted to hear the crack of the drumsticks on the snare drum. Some of the fills that I played were tasteful, accented rolls on the snare drum, and were integral parts of the songs. The drums,

The Reactions Love You

guitars, and all of the vocal parts ended up sounding very good. We spent a little extra time trying to liven up the sound of the bass, which at first sounded a little muted, but Tony did a fine job of getting the most out of it. After we had all pitched in to mix each individual track of the first song, it was just a matter of blending all of the tracks together for each song. Tony Mancino had an outstanding ear and needed very little input from Suppa or Baruch, who because they had written the songs, would have had the most say on the final mix.

By around 4:30 in the morning, Tony Mancino, with a big smile on his face, handed us the two-track master reel-to-reel tape. The recordings had come out great and he was proud of the work he had done. We were certainly grateful for his exceptional engineering and mixing skills, and for letting us slide on the extra costs. We left there with a very satisfying feeling of accomplishment. Our next step would be to transfer the reel-to-reel tape onto vinyl, so that we could release a record.

But that required money, which we did not have. Unfortunately, the beer sales scheme was a one-time shot. As usual, we had many more rivers to cross. But with the right attitude, and the right friends, a solution was always nearby.

I was the only one in the band who worked at a regular job. Three shifts. Breakfast, lunch and dinner. Each day as a busboy at a fancy health spa on Harbor Island. The pay was okay for a busboy position and the work was not terribly hard. I had saved enough to upgrade from the Kawasaki 100 motorcycle that I had ridden to the first Blue Waters gigs, to a magnificent 1972 Kawasaki 500 H-1, which was an extremely fast, very rare, two-stroke, three-cylinder motorcycle. The bike was so unusual and so cool that once when I ran out of gas on The Florida Turnpike, a bearded, patch-wearing biker on a Harley stopped to help me.

The Reactions Love You

I was very worried because I knew outlaw bikers didn't take kindly to Japanese bikes, or "rice burners" as they called them. When he saw it was an H-1, Kawasaki or not, he appreciatively said, "nice bike" and connected our motorcycles with a five-foot rope. He then towed me the 24 miles to the next service station at 70 miles per hour.

But the real money came from the help of some new friends from the scene, who fronted me some pot to sell. I started making significantly more than my busboy wages at the spa by selling ¼ oz. bags to almost everyone that worked there. Cooks, waiters, busboys, hosts, hostesses, and even the jazz band that played nightly, all were buying their weed from me. It was not my goal to be either a busboy or a small-time pot dealer, so as soon as I made enough to pay for the record, I quit both jobs.

Within one month of The Reactions finishing up at Music Recording Labs, with great pride, I announced that I would pay to produce our record.

Isaac and I weren't experts yet, but we at least understood the process a little better now and were confident that the second time around would produce better results. Instead of using Criteria Studios to master the record, we decided to take the two-track reel-to-reel tape to K&K Mastering Labs. With Official Release, some of the sound quality had deteriorated between the studio recording and the vinyl record. We suspected the loss occurred on the master disc, so we wanted to try someone else. K&K was also a lot cheaper than Criteria. This time, Isaac sat in on the job to help equalize (EQ) it and to make sure it captured the true sound of our recordings. When we brought the master disc to Miami Tape, we insisted on hearing what the mother plate sounded like before we sent the records to be stamped. That way if there was an issue with the sound on the vinyl we would know exactly what the culprit was. We made the right choice. The mother disc was a true, high-quality representation of the recording so we ordered 1,000 records to be pressed.

While we were waiting for the vinyl, one of my poker buddies from a regular game that I played at on Star Island on Thursday nights, Bruce Turkel, who owned a commercial art design company in Coconut Grove, volunteered to design our record cover. Bruce would always tell me that he just had a feeling that our record was going to be a big deal on a national scale. He wanted to help and didn't charge us a penny more than the costs of the materials. When I went to his office a week later to see the artwork, it blew me away.

The band had decided to title the record, *The Reactions Love You*. It was our way of saying thank you to all the people that had so enthusiastically supported us. We really did love you. Bruce's concept for the record cover was to design a black colored heart using strips of a waxed paper type of material that gave it a textured and uniquely creative feel to it. THE REACTIONS was written at the top of the cover, and LOVE YOU was inserted into the middle of the heart. The back cover was a picture of The Reactions at our first big gig opening up for The Ramones at The Agora Ballroom. Underneath the picture, handwritten, were the songs and credits. I was truly floored when he showed me what he had come up with. This record was going to be the complete product, with great artwork, great songs, and great recordings. I excitedly drove it straight to Miami Tape across town in Hialeah. In six weeks, the vinyl and covers would be ready and the world would finally be introduced to The Reactions.

An Offer We Can't Refuse

Our fans were as faithful and as enthusiastic as ever, and they appreciated the progress that the band was making. Oftentimes, a band will lose touch with what made them enjoyable in the first place, and their "progress" kills the band. I am certain you can think of many bands that sounded amazing at the beginning of their careers, but then **sucked** afterwards. Our progress resulted in a noticeable improvement, and our shows were now a minimum of one and a half hours of high-energy, sing-along, and dance-along songs. But we wanted more. We wanted the mass, mainstream audience, and believed that if given half a chance, we would earn that. Unfortunately, crossover acceptance came frustratingly slow in South Florida.

While we were waiting for our records to be ready, John Lennon was tragically murdered in NYC. I can remember exactly where I was when I heard the news, and clearly recall the nauseating feeling that engulfed me. John Lennon's music, and philosophy, transcended genres. So when a local promoter set up an impromptu memorial concert at Bayfront Park in Miami and invited The Reactions to play, we felt it was a responsibility and an honor to do so. That Sunday, more than 10,000 people showed up to mourn the passing of one of the world's most exceptional people. The promoter's thought was to have two progressive, original bands play. After all, who was more progressive than John Lennon? The Reactions and The Kids, with Bruce Witkin and Johnny Depp in the band, were the bands invited to play. The Kids went on first and played 45 minutes of their fabulous original songs. They received a politely warm

An Offer We Can't Refuse

reception for their effort. The Reactions were next. We were all very sad and angry that Lennon had been shot dead. Not to use that as an excuse, but we had been drinking for hours before The Kids even went on. When it was our turn to hit the stage, we were absolutely hammered. Our polluted condition would not have normally hindered us from getting through the set, but this was not our usual punk audience. The park was over-flowing with people, and it was apparent when we started playing that we were not what they were expecting. Being the optimists we were, we thought we would eventually win them over if we just kept on playing, but that just caused the crowd to get even more agitated. I could see Bruce Witkin with his bass guitar strapped on, motioning Isaac and Tony to get the fuck off the stage, and to do so quickly! So after maybe playing about six songs in total, we exited the stage to a nice chorus of boos, and "you suck," and were replaced by The Kids, who were met with an additional smattering of boos. They surprised everyone by immediately breaking into a brilliant set of Beatles songs played perfectly! Who would have thunk they knew so many Beatles songs? They sounded great and salvaged the beautiful memorial show.

That concert had a faint, but nevertheless tangible effect on all of us. Was it possible that our music was tailored for a much narrower audience than we had projected? We had always thought of ourselves as a rock and roll band…the next Beatles, not the next Sex Pistols or Ramones. We rationalized that we shouldn't be too concerned about bombing in front of an unmistakably closed-minded audience. But the seed of doubt was planted that day, even if only shallowly.

We decided to take some time off while the record was in production. Not only did we need the break, 'cause we were exhausted, but also figured audiences would be hungry to hear us play again and would want to buy our record even more if

An Offer We Can't Refuse

we laid low for a while. Nobody, except possibly Tony Suppa, would have ever imagined that this was actually the beginning of the end for us. Tony was getting major pressure from his family now. We still didn't pay too much attention to it because we thought it was just the usual parental crap of music being a dead-end journey, and that he was getting too old for this shit, blah, blah, blah. But it was more than that. Unbeknownst to us, Tony had been given an ultimatum by his father to get signed immediately to a record label or quit the band and join the family business. We had an amazing, exciting record coming out in six weeks. Without any uncertainty, we would then be signed to a major record label and embark on a national tour. Tony would surely wait for that.

We took four weeks off and then set up a Saturday night show at The New Wave lounge in Ft. Lauderdale. There was a real buzz in town about the upcoming record, and people were really starting to believe that The Reactions would be the local band to make it big. They were proud of us and wanted to be a part of it. The New Wave Lounge was packed probably beyond capacity, as the audience was squeezed in at the front of the stage and all along the long two walls that ran to the back of the room. In spite of the claustrophobic conditions, it seemed like everybody was feeling pretty good. We blasted through a one hour and thirty-minute set, and then came out and did thirty more minutes of cover songs as an encore, including punk versions of Motown classics, "When You Walk in the Room" and "Then She Kissed Me." Both of these songs are simple, intense, very passionate songs, and we played them as if we felt and believed every word, which in turn caused the audience to feel and believe it as well. We played "Magnificent Seven" and "Police on My Back" from The Clash, "Glad all Over" by Dave Clark Five, and an up-tempo, punk rock version of Tommy James and the

An Offer We Can't Refuse

Shondells' "I Think We're Alone Now." We gave it our all, and everyone that night felt as if they were part of something special.

That same night, I had gone to dinner with Tony and Isaac before the show, and I could swear that Tony was acting strange; he wasn't connecting to me in the way that he normally did and wasn't holding my eye gaze when we spoke. I noticed it, but since we're guys, I didn't make too much of it.

As it turned out, the next week, Tony unexpectedly quit the band. We tried to convince him to at least wait for the record to come out, but he wasn't even hearing us. Isaac, Johnny, and I discussed replacing Tony, but the harsh reality was that if we were going to continue as a band, we would have to replace Johnny as well. As important as he had been to the formation of The Reactions, Johnny was likely to remain a drag on the band. Neither Isaac nor I wanted to kick Johnny out of the band and neither of us wanted to quit on The Reactions either, but it had to be one or the other. And so I made the most difficult choice of my life and decided to pursue my plan B, which was to go to college while I was still young enough to do so. Isaac didn't even try and convince me otherwise.

We agreed to complete the record in the very outside chance that we would be miraculously discovered. We would then continue right from where we had left off. Before the record had even come out however, Tony made it clear that rejoining the band was no longer an option. No matter what.

The only thing left to do was to throw a giant, "goodbye" concert bash in Ft. Lauderdale, which we did on a Monday night at The Button on the Beach. The spacious bar was packed with an estimated crowd of over 1,200 people. The emotion in the room was palpable. I set a new high, or maybe I should call it a

An Offer We Can't Refuse

new low, for being totally wasted as I played. I played well and kept a smile on my face, but my true anger and despondency manifested itself when I unexpectedly asked Tony to let me sing "Roadrunner," which is a song written by Jonathan Richmond that we played from time to time. "Roadrunner" is a poetic song about the powerful effects of music and a cool car. This would be the last time that The Reactions would transport their audience to a better place, just as "Roadrunner" had so often transported me. I had never sung on stage before and wasn't even allowed to go near a microphone anymore. The only time I had ever grabbed a mike was to angrily berate a small audience at some shithole bar at the Hollywood Beach Boardwalk that The Reactions were playing at. I had yelled into Tony's mike that the only people in the bar that night were lesbians and rednecks. The lesbians were my friends, so they thought my outburst was funny. But the rednecks? Well, these rednecks were no friends of mine. What followed was a veritable bloodbath of violence. One of the rednecks jumped up on stage to confront me, so I punched him in the face. He fell to one knee, and before I could punch him again, Johnny swung his bass like an ax and caught him right on the head. The guy immediately started spurting blood from his head like a fountain! We assumed that the guy's friend, who was now also up on the stage, was going to attack us, so Isaac punched him. And that's when Isaac's good friend Paul, who was in the audience, got in on the action. Paul happened to have on him a pair of brass knuckles, so **he** jumped on stage and took Isaac's place hitting the guy in the face over and over again with the brass knuckles on. There was so much blood on that stage that I almost vomited. The two guys were carted off by paramedics, and we were asked never to come back to that bar. After that night, I was understandably forbidden from speaking into a microphone ever again.

An Offer We Can't Refuse

This night was different and Tony agreed to let me sing the song while he played my drums. I didn't even try and sing the correct words to the song. The audience seemed entertained, if not mildly amused, by my effort to make up my own lyrics to communicate my disappointment and anger for the reason that we had gathered that night. It was a bittersweet night and I cherished the opportunity to spend one more night up on stage with my best friends, my family...but the sadness was apparent.

A few days later, the cover artwork was ready to be approved by Isaac and me. On that same day, a small article came out in the entertainment section of *The Miami News* announcing the breakup of The Reactions. It read like an obituary. On the way to the printers, Isaac and I stopped at a newspaper vending machine (remember those?) and emptied out all the newspapers. When we got to Miami Tape, I got the impromptu idea to include the newspaper clip on the back of the record cover. Both Isaac and the printer gave me the green light to go for it. I then had another idea and excused myself to go outside to the parking lot. I began to light the article with a match till some of it burned away. Around the 3rd or 4th try, I achieved the effect I was looking for. I brought the burnt article inside and showed it to Isaac. For a moment, I thought we were both going to break out hysterically crying. Public bravado aside, we were devastated, and this article seemed to solidify the realization that it was truly over. Instead, with a pursed smile, Isaac shook his head and quietly said, "How fucking appropriate." And so, on the back of *The Reactions Love You* is a small, partially burnt article that encapsulates our brief, but exciting history. The black burn stains symbolize how in a flash, it can all disappear.

Isaac and I went through the motions of distributing the record in the same manner as our first record. Within a short period of time, without any marketing at all, over 300 of the records were

An Offer We Can't Refuse

purchased locally. Those vinyl records are all that remain of the mighty Reactions.

One can only wonder what we would have sounded like in another year or two. We were so young, and there was so much that we didn't know. Time would have cured that. What time didn't need to provide was chemistry, which is something you either have, or don't have. The Reactions had it.

We weren't the best musicians. Tony didn't sing like anybody else and he wasn't as attractive as singers usually are. But Tony was a great singer for The Reactions, and his face…was the proud face of The Reactions. Isaac often played basic bar chords and his leads were simple, melodic leads…but those simple power chords were what made the songs sound anthem-like, and his leads were what made the songs sound like beautiful songs, not ego-stroking, masturbatory guitar bullshit. Johnny Salton was a once-in-a-lifetime talent on lead guitar, but in The Reactions, he played a bass line that would have driven the songs through a concrete wall if necessary. My drumming… well, a 17-year-old drummer rarely gets invited to join the virtuoso musicians of Chick Corea. However, my particular set of skills were well-suited for The Reactions. I was fast as fuck, strong, and the songs sounded good the way I played them. Were we the best musicians? No. But were we the best fucking band? Many people believe that we could have been.

To paraphrase something I recently read on the Internet, "*The Reactions Love You* should have been a classic to be enjoyed by many 30 years ago, and not just by the few geeky record collectors that pay a fortune for it now." How true and how sad. It ended as abruptly as it had started.

The era of The Reactions was now over.

Joey Goes to College

I saw myself at college yesterday. I was broke, but surprisingly enough, definitely happy. My mind was solely on the courses I was taking at school and on the material I had to learn to do well on the exams. I wasn't worried about politics, the economy, or the horrible events happening around the world. I was aware of all those things, but I just wasn't worried about them. My blood pressure was perfect and my inner organs were not yet swollen from the abuses of our environment, or from my own self-inflicted abuses. I was thin, strong, and overflowing with joyous optimism. That's what I saw yesterday in hundreds of college students at Miami Dade College while I was on the way to a business appointment. I saw myself in them and wondered how I got from there to here so damn quickly.

After The Reactions disintegrated, I immediately started attending classes at the local community college. After two semesters and 21 easy credits under my belt, I decided it was time to transfer to a "real" college and enrolled at University of Florida. You might be wondering how a Quaalude-taking, hard-drinking, high school dropout, punk rocker like me can even get into a great college like the University of Florida? Well, I happen to be a **smart**, Quaalude-taking, hard-drinking, high school dropout, punk rocker! Before I dropped out of high school I had taken the SAT exam, which is the exam most colleges base their acceptance on, and already knew I had scored high enough to be automatically accepted at UF. And by high enough, I also mean that I took the test still high from smoking hash until 4 a.m. the night before. It was some outrageous Afghan black hash that got

College

you so much higher than normal pot, so I was still very buzzed when the test began at 7 a.m. In order to get the highest possible test score, many students take a PSAT exam (preparatory SAT exam) in 11th grade, enroll in SAT preparatory courses, and then take the SAT exam more than just one time in 12th grade. Your results are likely to improve the more times you take the exam. I took the SAT only once, without preparing for a single minute, and I was stoned when I took it. My score was far below my potential, but it was enough to get accepted, so I registered for summer session courses at the University of Florida.

By now I was not your typical 18-year-old college-bound boy. Not by a far cry. It was crazy to think, even unreasonable to believe that I even could assimilate myself into a college environment. I tried. I didn't even come close.

Before leaving for Gainesville, home of the renowned Florida Gators, I wanted to give a proper adieu to S. Florida, which to me meant partying for three days at a Holiday Inn on Collins Avenue with my girlfriend and a few friends. Our scheme was to pay for one night at a hotel and then keep one of the keys so we could go back and use the unoccupied room in the future. You could get away with that back then, and we had multiple keys from hotels up and down Collins Avenue to sneak into. From time-to-time we would barge in on someone already in the room, which was awkward, but for the most part, it was a great scam. For meals, since we didn't have much money, we would dine and dash. We felt like outlaws, like Bonnie and Clyde. I wasn't sure when I would have sex again while I was away at school, so Sonnie and I set a few records in those three days before I shipped out.

To kick the partying up a notch, or three, the day before the festivities began I was hired by my friend Paul, whom you've

College

already met, to buy a bottle of 100 Quaaludes at a pharmacy, by using a prescription that I obtained from a stress clinic that he owned. I then turned the pills back over to him so he could then sell those pills for an exorbitant profit. Got it? Stress clinics back then were a legal way to obtain Quaaludes the same way that pain clinics now are a legal way to obtain the narcotic Oxycontin. Both were, and still are, semi-legal drug trafficking organizations. My pay for the effort was that I got to keep ten of the Quaaludes. Worked for me! Late Sunday afternoon, when the three days were up, I said goodbye to my hopefully satiated girlfriend and took off for college with my brother Eli, who was in his last semester at Florida. I never turned in the remaining ninety ludes to Paul. Oops!

After five hours on the Florida Turnpike, we pulled in to my brother's girlfriend's apartment in Gainesville. Both of the girlfriend's roommates seemed to show some interest in me, so I invited them back to my apartment, where we started playing poker for quarter pieces of Quaalude. After about an hour of cards and Quaaludes, we stumbled onto the bed in my room, which was just a mattress thrown on the floor. In town two hours and I'm naked with two co-eds. I was going to **love** college! Actually, one of the girls was well on the way to passing out and asked me to take the contact lenses out of her eyes, which was not an easy task to accomplish high on Quaaludes. After I plucked out her lenses, she blacked out naked on my bed. That still left one semi–coherent, very horny girl, and I enthusiastically proceeded to set what I believe were some additional records on my first night at UF.

Classes began two days later and unfortunately, the events of the first day were the exception, not the rule for the three months of summer session. Things did liven up some a week later.

College

One of my baseball buddies from Beach High, Tito, drove up in an orange VW Jetta to stay with me for the remainder of the summer. I should mention that the VW was stolen. The owner of the car had given Tito the keys and told him to do whatever he wanted with the car just as long as he got the car out of South Florida, so that in two days he could report the car stolen and collect the insurance money. Being the geniuses we were, we decided we would borrow the car for the entire summer. To make matters worse, the starter was broken, so the only way to start the car was to push it and then pop the clutch, which we did for an entire week before we had a new starter and a badly needed new muffler installed at the local Midas shop. Before we had invested the $109 into the stolen car, and we were crazy enough to invest money into a stolen car, we had push started the loud, orange-colored car more than once in plain view of the Gainesville Police Department. Nerve-racking!

Other than occasionally driving around in a stolen car, I really did try to embrace college life. I went to classes and met up with friends at the local bars to chug beers, eat oysters, and meet the girls that attended UF. You know, typical college stuff. It just seemed like a giant step backwards for me. Even worse was my attempt to reconnect with friends that had joined fraternities. I'm not against fraternities. I am certain many lifelong friendships are established there, and I could see it as a fun way to get through college. It was just not for me. I needed rebellious excitement. I needed rock and roll music. So, I started hanging out by myself at some of the rock and roll bars just south of the university. There was nothing blatantly wrong with the bands that played there, but the music they played lacked any originality at all. Although original bands were not always fully appreciated in South Florida, at least we had them. You could go to a Big Daddy's Lounge and see Charlie Pickett playing live, with Johnny Salton on guitar, on almost any Saturday night. In

College

Gainesville, there was nothing of the sort. Charlie was eventually discovered by Peter Buck, the guitar player of REM, who produced Charlie's outstanding album, *The Wilderness*, and sent him off on an extensive tour of the United States. We always knew Charlie was something special, just as we always knew ex-Reactions Johnny Salton, who was now playing lead guitar in Charlie Pickett's band, was special. On Peter Buck's 2012 solo album, *Peter Buck*, Peter wrote and dedicated the song "So Long Johnny" to the deceased Johnny Salton. To revisit the question I posed earlier as to whether Johnny was a genius or a fuck up? He was definitely a little, or a lot, of both.

I was beginning to hate being in Gainesville. I couldn't find friends that I could relate to and I wasn't having any fun. And classes? Well, classes are never fun. To get a feel for the academics at UF, I had enlisted in two courses for that summer session: French and Calculus. I had really been into learning French during high school, and was one of the very few kids that understood that there was a big difference in the French language between oo and u, and è and e. The vast majority of high school students couldn't care less for the many subtle nuances in pronunciation that are essential to learn any foreign language. I loved all that crap and was therefore looking forward to studying French at college. Calculus also didn't concern me too much. I never had trouble with any math class, so I didn't even bother going to classes the entire first week. Keep in mind that during summer session, they complete a full 16-week program in only 12 weeks, so they cruise along quickly. And calculus isn't a joke. When I finally did show up for class, the first thing I noticed was that the entire front of the room was filled with Asian kids, replete with pimples and Coke bottle thick glasses. I thought to myself, "This is a bad omen." Sure enough, when the professor began to speak, he might as well have been speaking Korean. I was very far behind.

College

Both the French and the calculus courses were much more challenging than I had expected, and it took many weeks to catch up and get on track. By attending hours and hours of boring language labs and staying up late teaching myself calculus, I ended up passing both classes. Don't ask what my grades were. I passed.

I needed a break from my boredom and frustration, so mercifully, about a month after classes had begun, Isaac, Sonnie, and Rose picked me up on the way to go see The Clash at The Fox Theatre in Atlanta. The Reactions had broken up a year earlier, and I really missed hanging out with Isaac, Sonnie, and Rose. We always had a great time whenever we were together, which was often. I missed the whole South Florida scene really badly while I was in Gainesville.

As soon as we got to our hotel room, which was on Peach Street directly across from The Fox Theatre, from our window we could see Joe Strummer, the singer of The Clash, holding court in front of the theatre. He had a cleanly trimmed, short Mohawk, and was wearing a red, button-down, cowboy-style shirt with cut-off sleeves, and white pants tucked into his combat boots. For hours he was surrounded by people wearing red shirts or wearing red bandanas. We assumed it was a display of Mr. Strummer's socialist, or communist, political slant, but we didn't place a ton of importance on it. The Clash was truly our favorite band and we really believed The Clash was "the only band that matters," which was their marketing catch phrase. To this day, they are still my all-time favorite band. Seeing The Clash was a really big deal for us.

The Fox Theatre was spectacular. What a magnificent place to see a band, especially The Clash. But as soon as the concert started, I could tell something was wrong. It didn't sound like The Clash of *Sandinista* and *London Calling*, the albums that reflect the sublime progress of the band. The band was not tight at all. It sounded like they needed many more rehearsals to sound like The Clash that we all knew. Even worse, from my perspective, the drumming was awful! What happened to the jazz subtlety of *London Calling*? *London Calling* is definitely a punk record, but it is not what most people perceive punk rock to sound like. It is worth noting that *Rolling Stone Magazine* voted *London Calling* the number one album of the entire 1980's, ahead of many of the greatest bands that the world has ever known. The first time I listened to The Clash, I didn't even understand what I was hearing. I listened to "Safe European Homes," "Garageland," and "Janie Jones," and said to Isaac, as a matter of fact, "What is this?" I had been under the mistaken impression that punk rock was aggressive, tasteless music played by sub-par musicians. The songs I had just listened to were very well-written, excellently performed, and contained lyrics that tackled important issues. Once I opened myself up to the range of what punk rock really was, I thought to myself, "Oh, **that's** punk rock." I was hooked.

I tried to remain optimistic and was hoping that the band was having only temporary difficulties. I speculated that maybe the stage monitors had to be turned up or that the sound in the concert hall itself had to adjusted, but it never got any better. The Clash just totally sucked that night.

We later found out that the drummer, Topper Headon, had quit right before the start of that 1982 U.S. summer tour, or was busted for heroin possession, or was kicked out of the band for being a junkie…you choose which story you want to believe. We didn't have the Internet back then to know these things ahead of time. Before the set was too far along, I had figured out that it

College

was The Clash's original drummer, Terry Chimes, playing, and not Topper Headon. To be fair, Terry Chimes plays very well on the early Clash albums, but the band had progressed so much on the last three albums, and he was just not part of that progress.

Believe it or not, the concert itself, which was a giant disappointment, was not the most significant part of the evening. As we were stepping out of The Fox, there seemed to be some commotion and some muffled screaming. We could see some punks getting into it with some cops, but that was not unusual at a punk event, especially in the South. Before long, it was apparent that this was more than just a typical punk anarchist versus inflexible police officer's stand-off. There seemed to be a horde of people wearing red shirts and red bandanas running amuck in the streets. We crossed to the other side of Peach Street, where our hotel was, to avoid any trouble.

And fuck, fuck, fuck…that's when all hell broke loose! The fine City of Atlanta had called in the riot squad, which showed up in full riot gear, and were aiming to bust some punk rock skulls in. And that's exactly what they did. I personally witnessed an officer knock down a kid who was just walking in the street, and when the kid fell to the pavement, the officer proceeded to crack that boy's skull open with repeated full force swings of his hard, wooden baton. It could just as easily have been me. I saw a steady stream of blood flowing from his head and onto the street. The riot squad was being completely indiscriminate as to whose heads they were bashing in, because I certainly didn't witness any provocation to elicit such a radical response, and I was standing right there. Does wearing a red bandana and running in the streets chanting communist slogans warrant getting smashed in the skull? Most of the kids weren't even doing that. We were just trying to leave the concert. I thought about helping one of the kids that was getting his head bashed

College

in, but then came to the quick realization that I was a pussy. All kidding aside, I'm really not a total pussy, I just didn't want to get my own head cracked open, which is all that I would have accomplished. So I grabbed Sonnie and Rose (we had been separated from Isaac) and we got the hell out of there. The front doors of all the hotels, including ours, were locked, so we ducked into the alley behind the hotels.

We went in through the back door of a random hotel and guess who we ran into? That's right witches! Sitting around a large rectangular banquet table was none other than The Clash. The greatest rock and roll band in the history of the universe was chowing down on cold cuts and fried chicken while their fans were being brutally assaulted by the City of Atlanta riot squad right outside of their hotel doors. Joe Strummer was at the head of the table with Mick Jones sitting to his right, while Paul Simonon was across from Mick Jones. The drummer, Terry Chimes, was at the far end of the table. At the middle of the table sat some of the road crew and the road manager, who got up to inquire who we were, and how we got here. The band members appeared to be a little uptight and none of them were smiling, but they sat up higher in their chairs and their eyes got a little brighter when they saw Sonnie and Rose, who were both dressed in the provocative style that defines female punk rock fashion. Sonnie was wearing a short plaid skirt, ripped fishnet stockings and Doc Marten boots, and Rose was wearing a black leather mini-skirt, a ripped band T-shirt, and black Beatle boots. I happened to have a half-full pint of Jack Daniels in my hand as we walked in and offered to share it. Terry Chimes motioned my way, so I handed him the bottle as I sat down next to Mick Jones. Sonnie was very content to chat with Paul Simonon, whom I knew she had the hots for, while the cerebral Rose hit it off with Joe Strummer. Mick Jones made the mistake of asking me what I thought of the show. I hadn't really had a lot of time to process what I had just witnessed, so I just blurted out the unfiltered truth, "I didn't think you guys were very tight. What's wrong?"

Those were my exact words to Mick Jones. I was waiting for the response, which I was certain would clear everything up. **My** response that I would then follow up with after hearing **his** explanation would surely be, "Oh, **that's** what happened. That could happen to anyone!" I would then laugh and help myself to some cold cuts with my new buddy, Mick Jones of The Clash. But in actuality, his face morphed from dismayed, to insulted, to finally, capitulation, as he must have already known they had sucked that night. As he looked down and away, his exact words to me were, "I don't know."

That's it! That was the extent of my conversation with the great Mick Jones. I then wanted, better said, needed, some Jack Daniels, so I got up and went to hang out with Terry Chimes. I don't remember what we spoke about, but Terry and I hung out for a while shooting the bull and drinking the Jack; just two drummers, Terry Chimes, of **The Clash**, and me. How ridiculously fucking cool was that? I didn't want to overstay our welcome, so I got up to say good luck and goodbye to the band. Knowing the band world, staying too long would have implied certain things about what Sonnie and Rose would be willing to do, which neither of them wanted to. I was absolutely correct and we left as things were beginning to get a little awkward between the band and the girls.

The riot police were gone and it was safe now to walk over to our hotel, which had unlocked its doors. That night we ended up at the 688 Club, which was the cool, local punk club. We had a great time partying with the locals, and the next morning when we woke up, there were a few extra bodies lying around our hotel room. Before we got on the highway back to Gainesville,

College

we stopped for breakfast in town. We were a group of tattered, hungover punk rockers being served a Southern breakfast of eggs, grits, biscuits with gravy, and coffee by ladies with beehive hairdos and heavy Southern drawls, which was enough to remind us that we were still in the Deep South. We had had enough of "Southern hospitality" and just wanted to get the hell out of Georgia. Isaac, Sonnie, and Rose hung out with me in Gainesville, and after tubing down the Ichetucknee River on Sunday morning, they headed back home to South Florida. By Sunday night, I was alone again.

Soon after The Clash concert I was again climbing the walls with boredom. I had to establish some kind of social life. For many years, my music and social life had been one and the same, so I answered a "drummer wanted for an original music band" ad taken from the bulletin board at Burrito Brothers on 13th Street and University Avenue. Original music is obviously a wide category, but original was what I wanted, so I called the phone number on the flyer and made arrangements to meet up with a guy named Bob Fetz, who conveniently lived just 20 blocks north of me, in a trailer park on 13th street. Tito and I were still sharing the stolen Jetta, but he always had first dibs on using it, so I pedaled my bike to Bob's trailer home.

Bob was a skinny, innocuous looking guy maybe a year or two older than me, and he played me some recordings of a band that he and a guy named George Tabb had formed. It was pretty standard hardcore, Minor Threat/ Black Flag sounding stuff, which though I enjoyed both of those bands, I had no interest in playing serious hardcore punk rock. What sold me were the lyrics. They were hilarious! The music sounded wild and edgy, but it was obvious that these guys didn't take themselves overly serious. A few days later, Bob, George, and I ran through some of the songs. I had immediately taken a liking to both of them

College

and therefore accepted their invitation to join their band, which was called Roach Motel.

Roach Motel went on to gain some infamy by touring with some top national punk bands and by releasing some good local records, which today have some value as collector's items. But when I played with the band during the summer of 1982, I was just enjoying the moment. We played at local bars and even did a three-night engagement in Daytona Beach, where surprisingly enough, we received a cordial reception. People in Florida, and Northern Florida in particular, do not listen to Minor Threat, Black Flag, or any punk bands. They listen to The Allman Brothers, Peter Frampton, Bachman, Turner, Overdrive, and so on. Today, thirty-five years later, the play list is still most likely the same. Roach Motel playing one-hour sets of original hardcore thrash songs such as "More Beer" should have been dead on arrival. But as I mentioned, we didn't take ourselves inordinately seriously. The music was tight and energetic, and the lyrics were entertaining, especially if you were young and looking to get drunk and have some fun. I would have taken that any day over listening to yet another band play Journey songs.

So college was finally going okay, and I was having fun as the drummer of Roach Motel, but I had no intention of returning to back-ass Gainesville for the fall semester. Gainesville was just not for me. I did however want to receive the credits for the two courses I had taken, which required I pass each of the two final exams. To complicate matters, Roach Motel received a massive break by being asked to open for Black Flag in South Florida, which was scheduled for the same day as the calculus final exam. Nothing in the world would have stopped me from playing that gig, so I came up with a plan that would allow me to take the final exam and to also make it to the show. Unfortunately, the plan went awry, and because of it, I would

College

end up never speaking with any of the guys from Roach Motel ever again. Even if they would have given me the chance to explain, my story would have sounded preposterous. As it turned out, they never even gave me the chance. Sadly, Bob Fetz passed away in July of 2017, so he will never know what happened. I do hope that George Tabb, after reading this, finally understands why I never made it to the Black Flag show. It was not a very good day for me. As a matter of fact, it ranks up there as one of my worst ever.

Black Flag and the Turnpike Killer

For those of you unaware, Black Flag is one of the greatest American punk bands ever. They are literally the gold standard. Their frontman, Henry Rollins, is a rock and roll icon. It was a really big deal for Roach Motel, of Gainesville, Florida, to be picked as the opening act for Black Flag's first ever South Florida appearance. To me, it was only a minor complication that my calculus final was from 11 a.m. to 1 p.m. on the same day as the gig, and the band needed to be in South Florida, which is about a five-hour car ride from Gainesville, by 4 p.m. My plan was to have the rest of the band leave at 10 a.m. with all of the equipment, and I would depart after my exam. We were scheduled to go on stage at approximately 8 p.m.

I stayed up the entire night cramming for the final exam. I drank a pot of coffee and took over-the-counter NoDoz and Vivarin pills to stay alert. At 10:15 the next morning, after maybe 3 hours of sleep, I got on my bicycle and pedaled to the auditorium where the test was being administered. I was ready to go when the test began at 11, and by quarter to one, I was finished. It's good to be 18. Even after the long, long night of learning the difficult material, and the pressure of having to pass the important final exam, I felt fine, fresh as a spring flower.

Tito had graciously agreed to let me use the stolen Jetta to travel to Hallandale for the show, so I packed my drumsticks, cymbals, and all the Quaaludes that I had left, and hit the road. Other than the three I shared with the two coeds on my first night in Gainesville, I hadn't taken another single Quaalude. I had sold a

Black Flag and the Turnpike Killer

few for some beer money, but it was always my intention to pay Paul for his pills. I was so stoked, so excited to play the Black Flag show, that the ludes were the last thing on my mind.

My IQ, at a minimum, is at least average. In a short period of time, I had basically taught myself an entire semester of college calculus, but yet, I had no qualms about driving a stolen car 330 miles across the State of Florida? What the fuck was I thinking? I had done plenty of stupid, misdemeanor types of hijinks, but this was full on grand theft auto, with a little insurance fraud thrown in for good measure. If caught, jail time was a certainty. I was 5'10", with barely any facial or body hair yet, and weighed only 152 pounds. I would not be going too far out on a limb by saying that behind bars, I'd be considered quite a catch, a tasty morsel, if you will. Jail would not have been a pleasant place for me. Obviously, I wasn't thinking about those pesky details. I was focused on getting back on stage and back into the limelight.

The first thirty minutes on I-75 South were uneventful, but no sooner had I reached Ocala, the engine started making some funny noises. Not ha-ha funny, but rather, clank, boing, clang funny. It sounded like the engine was on its way to seizing up, and when smoke began to billow from underneath the hood, that's exactly what happened. The car was dying. I managed to pull over to the side of the road, and then a wave of panic swept over me. If I got caught with the car now, I would be in very serious trouble! After calming down, I asked myself to think what a crafty criminal would do in this situation. Should I leave the car where it was, or should I try and hide it in the grass beyond the shoulder of the road? Those were the decisions that would determine if my life as I knew it would take a dramatic, drastic turn for the worse, or if this would one day make for an entertaining, close-call story. I decided to pull about 20 feet past the shoulder on a grassy embankment where the car was not obviously visible from the road. Rats. Did that just make the car even more obviously suspicious? Florida is as flat as a pancake, so the car was still visible, but just not as easily. That's where I left it. I grabbed the cymbal bag with all my stuff in it and started wiping fingerprints off of the car. Both Tito and I had our fingerprints on file with the Florida Department of Law Enforcement, so if they found our fingerprints on the car, they would easily find us, and we would have some explaining to do. Before you go picturing that Tito and I were hardened criminals, that wasn't the case it all. Tito had been arrested a few months earlier for the badass crime of not paying a driving ticket. I was with Tito that night, and it shames me to admit that we got caught running out without paying for a six-pack of beer at a convenience store on NE 19th Ave. The clerk jumped over the counter like a gazelle and wrote down our license plate number. A few moments later, a North Miami Beach cop pulled us over, and when he ran our driver licenses, discovered that Tito had an arrest warrant outstanding for not paying a traffic ticket. He let us slide for stealing the beer, but hauled Tito off for the unpaid ticket. I also had been arrested only a few weeks earlier for stealing a few sirloin steaks from an Albertsons Supermarket. Damned they looked good! The charges were quickly dropped, but my fingerprints remained on file. So, as I had seen on countless cop shows, I quickly wiped down the entire car, and then took my place on the side of I-75 with my thumb out to hitch a ride.

Those ten minutes of waiting on the side of the turnpike within sight of the broken down, stolen Jetta felt like ten years. I thought to myself, "Thank you God!" when an 18-wheel trucker finally stopped to pick me up. After I told the driver where I was headed, he apologized and told me he was only able to take me the 20 miles or so to where the turnpike begins and I-75 veers off west towards Tampa, where he was headed. I needed to get as

Black Flag and the Turnpike Killer

far away from that stolen Jetta as quickly as possible. That trucker had no idea how grateful I was for that short ride, and though I'm certain he has long forgotten me, I will never forget the man that basically served as my get-away driver that day.

As promised, he dropped me off on the side of the road where I-75 splits away from the turnpike. I hopped out of the 18-wheeler's cabin and immediately began to walk back towards Florida's Turnpike, where I needed to be. My immediate observation was that these highways were definitely not designed for pedestrians. I was walking where it was not intended for people to be walking. It was a really shitty, sinking, depressing, and scary feeling as cars whizzed past me at 80 miles an hour. How was it possible that I was even in this situation? My next observation was that fuck, it takes a long time to walk somewhere that would take two minutes in a car. The walk to the turnpike took almost 40 minutes. It was up grassy hills, on long loopy curves, and over barriers designed to corral cars. The Central Florida sun was blazing hot that day, and for a few moments, I was certain that buzzards were circling above me. I finally made it to the southbound lane of the turnpike and stuck my thumb out to commence hitchhiking again. Almost immediately, a Florida State Trooper with his police lights flashing, pulled up next to me. That's it. I was busted! My worst nightmare was about to become a reality. Instead of opening up that evening for the premier punk band in America, I would spend the week in jail. And that would only be the beginning of my troubles and misery. The trooper however, simply advised me that the only place I was allowed to hitchhike was on the on-ramps. I was certainly not going to argue and was happy he did not offer to give me a ride, because I wasn't in the mood at the time to make small-talk with a cop. I was relieved that the stolen car obviously hadn't yet been found, so I said, "Thank you sir,"

Black Flag and the Turnpike Killer

and started walking towards the entrance ramp. I was even more worried now that I would get busted if they found the car.

It was around 3 p.m., and by my optimistic calculation, if I got lucky with rides, I could still make it to The Black Flag gig on time. After fifteen long and lonely minutes, I decided it didn't make sense to hitchhike on an entrance ramp that saw one car every five minutes, so I threw caution to the wind and started to hitchhike on the actual turnpike itself. I weighed the odds of the same trooper catching me illegally hitchhiking versus the consequences of the Jetta being found while I was still on foot on the turnpike and decided a hitchhiking citation was better than a grand theft auto felony conviction. It took an additional 45 minutes of waving my thumb, but a guy finally stopped to offer a ride. I got in his car and within about five minutes, I could tell that this was not a normal, well-adjusted man. To this day, I still believe it was his intention to either rape me, kill me, or both.

He looked to be about 40 years old, dressed kind of plain, with sandy brown hair that was cut short and conservatively. He didn't try to lay a finger on me and did not say anything suggestive, but I sensed he was building the courage to do both. His odd conversation and strange mannerisms did not match his conservative appearance, and that creeped me out and worried me. As we drove along, he asked me if I wanted to smoke a joint of some Gainesville Green, and I said sure, why not. I was doing my best to build some kind of rapport with him. After we finished the pungent joint, he wanted to stop at the next service station to get something to drink. At the service station, he insisted on having the boys that worked at the service station fill up his car with gas and clean his windshields. As soon as I saw the way he was behaving at the service plaza, I should have looked for another ride. He wasn't blatant or rude, and maybe I was just high as hell, but he was really fucking weird.

Black Flag and the Turnpike Killer

Considering the position I was in, I decided that I would take a chance that this guy would end up being just a harmless creep, and not a cold-blooded killer, so when he asked me to buy a six-pack of beer for the ride, I complied and got back in the car.

Disturbingly, that became his pattern. He stopped at every service plaza along the way and made a big to-do about having the attendants, who were all teenaged boys, top off the tank with gas and clean the windshields. The time dragged on, and what should have been a three-hour drive stretched to four hours. It was now pitch-dark outside and the guy seemed to be getting aggravated that he was not making the progress with me that he had possibly hoped for. We were getting close to the Hollywood exit, which was where I needed to get off to get to the Black Flag concert on Ocean Drive and Hallandale Beach Blvd. I now had no chance of making it on time unless he took me the whole way, so I took a risk by telling him point-blank, that if he drove me all the way to the club, I was 100% certain I could get him laid by either a girl, or a guy. My insinuation that he might be gay incensed him! When he dropped me off a few minutes later at the Hollywood exit and sped off, I breathed a giant sigh of relief. It was more than just a sigh. I outright laughed out loud. On one hand, I was unlikely to make it to the gig in time to open for Black Flag, and that sucked. On the other hand, I hadn't been arrested for driving a stolen car, sodomized, or murdered! I had plenty to be grateful for.

It took two more rides to get to Ocean Drive from the turnpike exit. I had stopped looking at the time, but I believe it was at around 9:30 that I arrived at the club. The guy who gave me the final ride, Gary Lambert, whom I have remained good friends with, recognized me from Reactions days, and also happened to be on the way to the Black Flag show. I didn't divulge too much

Black Flag and the Turnpike Killer

to him. I told him only that it been a long day and that I certainly appreciated the ride.

You would think that at this point I could just have a beer and enjoy watching Black Flag. But my ordeal was not quite over just yet. The first people that saw me get out of Gary's car were George and Bob from Roach Motel. They were absolutely devastated and heart-broken to have not opened for their idols, Black Flag. They were so disappointed in me that they only managed something to the effect of "How could you…?" I attempted an explanation, but also had trouble stringing together a coherent sentence to explain the events of the day. They quickly lost their patience, and dishearteningly walked away. I would have attempted again to explain, but I was then forcibly grabbed and thrown violently against a parked car!

Let me recap the previous 24 hours: I had stayed up all night drinking coffee and popping stimulant pills to cram all-night for a difficult calculus exam. I then drove, and then ditched a stolen car that broke down on Florida's Turnpike, forcing me to hitchhike for almost eight hours to get to Hallandale, to a gig that I ended up missing anyway. My last ride on the turnpike was from a guy who could have possibly been a sexually deviant killer, and now, Paul, the ex-bouncer turned stress clinic operator that I had misappropriated a few Quaaludes from, who happened to be at the Black Flag show, wanted to beat the shit of me! Are you with me?

I didn't think I stood much of a chance fighting Paul. He was a violent man and I had seen his handy-work first-hand and up-close more than once. But I wasn't scared of him that night. While he had me jacked up against the car, I calmly apologized to him and told him that I had most of his Quaaludes on me, and that it was never my intention to rip him off. I knew that Paul could never let me get away with ripping him off, because that would give off the signal that he could be taken advantage of. But I also knew Paul was honorable. If I gave him back the ludes, or at least paid for them, he could save face, and I could save mine. So, I handed him the 50 or so pills that remained and offered him the $36 that were in my pocket. Technically it wasn't "most" of the pills and that still left me about $200 short. Just when Paul was weighing whether or not to punch me in the face, my good buddy Isaac Baruch, who was also Paul's good friend, and also just happened to be there that night, convinced him to leave me alone. Paul hesitated a moment, and then smiled and told me never to pull a stunt like that again, and we all went inside Finder's Lounge to finally enjoy that well-deserved beer as we watched Black Flag play.

Paying Dues

Paying dues sucks. That's what I did from September of 1982 till August of 1984. The next five chapters are dedicated to everybody that has paid their dues. To the artists and musicians that were dead-ass broke, but rather than give up, swallowed their pride and moved into their mothers' garages. To the doctors that worked 36-hour shifts to get through their residencies. To the entrepreneurs, that at great personal risk, decided to forsake the comfortable path in order to create their own success. To the nurses, chefs, writers, plumbers, cabinet makers, research scientists, insurance agents, boxers, stockbrokers, MMA fighters, radio DJ's, engineers, film-makers, actors, teachers, athletes, producers, etc., etc. Just about everybody who has become somebody, at one point or another, has had to pay dues. Paying dues is tough, but since nothing worthwhile in life comes easily, paying dues is very necessary. My life sucked in 1982, it sucked in 1983, and it sucked for half of 1984. But then all of a sudden, what's the exact opposite of sucked? Oh yeah, life became fucking awesome again! I was finally where I belonged, touring the United States with an up and coming nationally recognized band, being interviewed on radio stations and by fanzines, and having glorious sex again. I missed all of those things. I loved playing good music on stage, I enjoyed being appreciated for playing well, and I loved the benefits that went along with playing and looking good. But Battalion of Saints was still two long, dues-paying years away.

Paying Dues

I had left for college thinking that I get my life back on track and have a college experience that would lead to a career that was both interesting and well-paying. I quickly found out that I couldn't fucking stand the college experience. I found it to be an antiseptic bubble, completely insulated from the real world. Even worse, I felt as if I was the only one who felt that way.

I still believed that college would uncover opportunities that at this point, I didn't even know existed. I'm not exaggerating. I literally had no idea what college would do for me, but it had to be better than the jobs that I was qualified for in the help-wanted section of the newspaper. I had already worked at a dry-cleaning store, at a supermarket, as a bus boy, as a day laborer, and as a cable TV salesman, which was silly, cause who would ever pay to watch TV? I didn't mind doing any of those jobs, but the pay was not very much at all. In an effort to make just a little more money, I once even answered an ad to join an escort service. A friend of mine from the baseball team tagged along for moral support, and together, we interviewed at the agency. Surprisingly enough, the jobs were offered to us and we signed employment agreements, lying that we were both 18 years of age, when in reality, I had just turned 17, and my buddy Mark, the catcher on the baseball team, was only 16. We both quit as soon as we found out that our "dates" would not be with women. How naive of us! When American Gigolo came out a year later, I remember thinking, "Hey, that was **my** idea!" Those were the jobs available for someone like me. Surely, there had to be more opportunity out there.

I didn't have any money saved up, so I reluctantly moved back in with my parents while I enrolled at Miami Dade Community College (MDCC) again. I couldn't have cared less for the college experience, but I still wanted the college education. Thankfully, I had the full support of my parents who were willing to help in

Paying Dues

whatever way they could. A roof over my head and free food was a good thing. For work, I got a job as a waiter at Nadines restaurant in North Miami Beach. I was not a very good waiter, but management put up with me. Since I was signed up for a full schedule at MDCC, putting up with me, and a paycheck, was all that I required from my employer.

I now needed to find a band to play with. My mental psyche was directly related to whether or not I was playing in a band, and whether the band was any good. When The Reactions ended, I was completely devastated and depressed. The more time that passed that I was not playing in a good band, the more depressed I became. I did what I had to at school, but there was no skip to my step, and no joy in my eyes.

Back in Miami now, I was at least jamming with the musicians who hung out at Sync Studios, but nothing clicked. Maybe it was a result of my own insecurities, but at school I didn't fit in with the other students, and in the music world, I felt alienated for the opposite reason; because I was a student. After being the center of attention for so long, it was not very pleasant to feel left out.

Isaac Baruch of The Reactions had formed, and was the lead singer, of a band called The U.S. Furys. They were straightforward rock and roll, and every song was very good and very catchy. They sounded like a cross between Generation X (Billy Idol's first band) and John Cougar Mellencamp. They were really good! It is remarkably difficult to write even an acceptably good song, but Isaac had the ability, the gift, to write **great** songs in any genre. When the drummer of The U.S. Furys quit, Isaac asked me to join the band. I told Isaac that I would join him if he would find another lead singer for the band. I loved Isaac, and as desperate as I was to join a good band, I didn't want to hitch myself to The U.S. Furys if Isaac remained as the lead singer. Isaac had a decent voice and enough charisma to be a frontman, but I felt that inevitably, his vocal shortcomings would put a cap on our success. When Isaac insisted on remaining the lead vocalist, although it greatly disappointed me, I instead joined The Spinouts, whom I thought at least had the potential to succeed on a national level. I did manage to get The Spinouts to NYC in late 1983, where a harsh recession, freezing cold weather, and a pestiferous band member tested our resolve. All I can tell you is that everything happens for a purpose. The Spinouts got me to New York City, which served to open my eyes nice and wide open. It was a monumental experience, although, of course, at the time I couldn't have cared less for the "experience."

Almost immediately after joining The Spinouts I started to get my personal groove back. We were headlining and attracting audiences from day one, and the emotional dark clouds began to lift off of me. I am the type of person that will stop at nothing to succeed, so I put 100% of my effort into helping this band succeed. To be sure, The Spinouts were not in the same league, the same anything, as The Reactions, but not only was I resolved to let the past stay where it belonged, but I also believed that The Spinouts stood a shot at commercial success. The band members were good looking and the music was lively and poppy. To help things along, I shared with The Spinouts many of the same concepts that I had learned with The Reactions. I insisted that we rehearse as many hours as possible so that when we played live we could focus on playing passionately, rather than having to think about the notes we were playing. It worked. Spinout shows were energetic and very entertaining.

The Spinouts were the perfect project for me. I needed to stay put locally so that I could attend college, but I also needed to be in a band that I could be proud of, and that at least had the

Paying Dues

potential to succeed. I was proud to be in The Spinouts, and at least for now, we had no plans to leave South Florida.

Spinouts members Steve Lambert, George Respeto, and Jack "Stack Jones" Stone conducted their rehearsals at Sync Studios, where I was already hanging out, so finding each other was easy. Sync Studios was more than just a place where local bands rehearsed for $5 per hour, it was also a cool "scene." Although bands seriously rehearsed and seriously recorded there, it was also a party place where alcohol, Quaaludes, and girls flowed abundantly. The original music scene was a close-knit community and we were always trying to help each other out, so more than one person told me that The Spinouts were sounding good and that they needed a drummer. The original drummer, Randy Blitz, quit after only one gig with the band after he witnessed Jack Stone throw a beer bottle at the drummer of Lords of The New Church while Lords of The New Church was playing at The Agora. I was at that show and had wondered what kind of an asshole would throw a glass bottle at a defenseless band. Although I didn't find out until years later, turns out that Jack was that asshole.

The Spinouts in turn, knew that I was available, because well, everybody knew I was looking for a permanent band. Before we rehearsed as a band for the first time, the bass player, George, agreed to come over my house after I had finished my morning session at MDCC, and patiently taught me ten Spinout songs. Some were originals and others were recycled, obscure, old rockabilly songs such as "20 Flight Rock" and "Brown Eyed Handsome Man." George was a skilled bass player, was very good looking, and was upbeat and enthusiastic about the band. Before those three hours were up, we were sounding as if we had been playing together much longer. Sure enough, at our first

Paying Dues

full band rehearsal it was immediately obvious that the chemistry was there.

Jack Stone was the brains behind the sound of the band and a very proficient guitar player. Jack wore his red hair in a perfect pompadour, and his pleated slacks, rockabilly style shirts, and cowboy boots completed his polished image. On stage he was a mad man, both very energetic and very entertaining. His jazz-oriented style of guitar was well-suited for rockabilly, which was the style of music that The Spinouts were modeled on. The Stray Cats, as a three–piece band where the drummer used only a snare drum and a ride cymbal, found monstrous success with their throwback traditional rockabilly sound. The Spinouts were looking to expand upon that by keeping the rockabilly foundation but emphasizing the "rock" part by having four band members instead of three and using a complete drum kit. We weren't trying to imitate the Stray Cats and didn't sound like them. We were a Psychobilly band, which is a style of music fusing rockabilly, punk rock, rock, and rhythm and blues.

The singer was Steve Lambert, coincidentally the older brother of the same Gary Lambert who had given me the final ride to the Black Flag gig on my unnerving last day at the University of Florida. Steve was the frontman whose high cheek bones and chiseled body more than made up for his limited vocal range.

When we played on stage, the band looked like a band. We all strived to have an "image" that oftentimes, local bands sadly lack. We put some thought into the pants, shirts, shoes, and accessories that we wore and made sure that our hair looked like some effort had been put into it. Isaac Baruch's Furys also took their images seriously, so every time The Spinouts and The U.S. Furys played on the same bill, it didn't feel like a local show; it was more as if two out-of-town bands were playing a concert.

Paying Dues

Both bands had their eye on making it in Los Angeles or New York City, not just Miami.

As it turned out, neither band stayed in Florida very long. By fall of 1983, both Isaac and I finally followed through on our Reaction's era plans to reach NYC. The Furys arrived in September of 1983 and The Spinouts made it up one month later. I became very good friends with Ricky Beck Mahler, the bass player of The Furys, and Ricky was one of the few friends that I remained close with whether I was in the world of music, college, or Wall Street. I eventually founded Circus Of Power with Ricky (and Alex Mitchel) in 1986 and wrote the song "Dream's Tonight" on the very first day that I moved in with him into his Lower East Side apartment on 12th Street between Avenues C and D. This was before the Lower East Side had been gentrified, and I could hear police sirens and loud disturbances right outside my second story window. To keep my sanity, I grabbed Ricky's guitar and composed "Dreams Tonight" from start to finish. The song begins, "We could be far away, somewhere in Paris or in Spain." Alex Mitchel captured perfectly in the lyrics what I was feeling at the time, and the song immediately became a mainstay of Circus of Power sets. But, I'm getting a little ahead of myself.

Back in Florida, The Spinouts were playing for larger audiences, and I was busy at school racking up credits. I did not want to prolong my stay at Miami Dade Community College any longer than necessary. I thought of it as a prison sentence, and just wanted to do my time, earn the credits, graduate, and move on. I went to the classes that required attendance and skipped the classes that didn't. I never even bothered to buy all of the required textbooks. I would go into the bookstore before an exam and read the required material right there on the floor of the bookstore. Then, I would return the book to the shelf and go

Paying Dues

take the exam. I maintained a solid B+ average, which is nothing to brag about because the nickname for MDCC was "13th grade." I had no interest in an Ivy League type of education and therefore, was at the perfect school for my circumstances.

Although I didn't go out of my way to look any different than the rest of the students, just dressing and looking "rock and roll" made me stick out, which was a two-edged sword. One of the classes required in order to graduate was Data Processing. The professor seemed cool and told us that anybody who could pass his exams without coming to class was welcome to try. Perfect.

For the final exam, which was scheduled for a Thursday, I did the same thing as I had done for the mid-term exam that I had scored a B on. I sat on the bookstore floor for about an hour and read the course book. But when I went to take the final exam, there was nobody there! The auditorium was deserted. I wanted to puke. I ran to the professor's office in a complete panic and happened to catch him just as he was stepping out.

"What happened to the final exam? It was supposed to be today," I stammered.

The professor looked at me and answered, "The test was moved to Tuesday. I announced it in class two weeks ago."

I confessed that I hadn't been to class and was concerned that the final exam counted for a large part of the final grade.

And then, the weirdest thing happened. He asked me my name, and when I told him, he said "Oh," as if he recognized it. He looked up my name on his already filled out and completed grade chart, and then smiled and said, "I gave you an A for the course. I'm sure you would have gotten an A on the final."

Paying Dues

That was a really strange thing to do, as he obviously had no basis for it, and it was very, very unexpected. I looked at him as if he were pulling my leg and said, "Really?"

"I gave you an A. Have a great summer."

As bizarre as it was, without that break I would have been forced to take an additional semester in order to graduate, which would have probably changed the course of my musical future. I believe in this case, my unique look worked to my advantage.

The Spinouts were playing at small local bars like 27 Birds in Coconut Grove and Flynn's on Miami Beach, and the shows were fun and exciting. We were really packing them in. The best local rock club, The Agora, was already gone and replaced by a gentleman's club, which is still there today. The fact that The Agora couldn't make it, but a strip club is flourishing, speaks volumes about South Florida.

Our popularity got our picture pasted on the front cover of *The Miami News* Lifestyle Section. The article was more about fashion than music, but hey, any publicity is good publicity. The newspaper had a big picture of the band posing like "bad boys" on a pile of custom rims at Hub Cap Heaven on State Road 441. We also made it to local TV as the featured band of The Ed Rich Rock Show. We were interviewed by the host of the show, Ed Rich, and then played a live set. Johnny Carson it wasn't, but it was TV, and it was great publicity.

Following the same blueprint as The Reactions, we were now ready to record and release a record. We decided to record at Sync Studios, which had a very good 24 track recording studio. We trusted that our friends that owned Sync, Hal Spector, Frank

Paying Dues

Falestra, and Luciano Delgado, would take good care of us, and they did. They charged us a reasonable $35 per hour fee, and the recordings, engineered by my longtime school friend Michael 'Mac' McNamee, came out good. Not fancy or overly produced, but more than good enough to serve as a first record. Paying for it was easier this time. The money we earned from gigs was enough to pay for the recording and for the records. We didn't have to sell beer to raise money like The Reactions had done.

The 12-inch, four-song Spinouts record came out during the summer of 1983. Two of the songs, "Blue Jean Bop" and "Hurricane" had mainstream FM Radio potential. We even pictured the MTV videos with pretty, pony-tailed girls in bellowing 50's style dresses dancing and swooning around us as we played the songs like teen idols. Anyway, that was the general idea. For that to ever really happen, it was clear that we needed to get to NYC. I only needed a handful of credits to graduate with an AA degree, so I decided to take the Fall 1983-84 semester off to work on finally getting to NYC.

I will now illustrate the great power of positive thinking: I considered it a fait accompli that three completely broke band members from South Florida (Steve was the only one with any money) would somehow get to NYC, find and pay for a place to live, and showcase at the local rock clubs. Fucking **NYC**! Happy, shiny people arrive daily by the busload, only to be swallowed up by that mean, nasty, dirty hellhole that is New York City. As far as I was concerned, it was a done deal.

The Spinouts were going to NYC!

New York City

How does one explain New York City to a person who has never been there? For starters, if you are not in NYC or Los Angeles, you are nowhere. What? Surely I jest! Unfortunately, I'm not exaggerating. However cool you think your city is, it's not. However good you think your restaurants are, they aren't. That's you Toronto, that's you San Francisco, and that's you Boston, Seattle, and Chicago. And that's especially you if you don't live in any one of those great North American cities. Music, plays, art, don't compare anywhere else. If you are not the absolute best at whatever it is that you are doing, the good folks in NYC will quickly be aware of it, and you are done. If you are weak, people will target you and prey on you. If you're tough, you're not tough until you are New York City tough. It's both a physical and a mental toughness. If you go to New York City as a tourist, it's not the same thing. I love visiting New York City, and although I can only afford NYC in small, limited doses, I do cherish the times I'm there and it is when I feel most alive. But a tourist sees things merely through a visitor's eyes. Moving to New York City to make it as an artist of any sort such as a musician, chef, painter, fashion designer, etc., poses a whole different level of difficult challenges. As I've mentioned, and you already knew anyhow, busloads of people arrive everyday in NYC to make their dreams come true, and everyday, just as many buses leave full of people that have been chewed up and spit back out. The reason that bands **still** have to go to LA or NYC to be discovered, is that if you're a band, and not eventually in NYC or LA, you are nowhere, and you probably won't ever be discovered.

New York City

From the time that I was 17, I understood that my journey to succeed wouldn't even begin until I had reached New York. I was far from tough and I was far from polished, but I was up for the challenge and I was up for the fight. I was now 20 years old and still stuck in Florida. That was about to change.

After being together and playing out regularly for the past 13 months, The Spinouts were sounding as good as we were going to sound and looking as good as we were going to look. Jack Stone had written another handful of original songs, which the band had worked on to complete. The new songs were a bit more complex, but I wasn't totally convinced that they made us a better band. Regardless, a band only needs one or two hits to get established, so as a band, we were ready to take our shot.

The first thing that we needed was money. Jack, George, and I were completely broke, and apartments in New York City were very, very expensive. Steve Lambert, the only one of us with some money in the bank, was definitely not going to bankroll this costly, long shot venture. So we turned to what many people in South Florida were already involved with: marijuana. Miami was a major gateway to the rest of the United States for marijuana. In fact, it was so prevalent, that if you lived in South Florida in the 80's it was difficult to not know at least one person involved in the marijuana trade.

The most common way that marijuana entered South Florida was by sea. A large boat, referred to as a mother ship, would depart South America filled with marijuana and rendezvous with smaller, faster boats, referred to as go fast boats, which would then transport the contraband to crews waiting at waterfront houses scattered throughout South Florida. It was difficult for the insufficiently funded Drug Enforcement

New York City

Administration (DEA) or Coast Guard to do anything about it because in the early 80's they were inadequately equipped to do so. The go-fast boats, which typically were expensive, very fast Cigarette boats, could easily outrun anything that the Coast Guard had. After the crew had unloaded the pot from the Cigarette boat, a truck would then haul the merchandise to a central location for further distribution out of the state. It was a well-organized, very profitable operation. Contrary to common belief, the organizations that controlled the marijuana trade were not violent at all and ran their operations as reasonable business ventures. It wasn't until cocaine began to dominate South Florida a few years later that everything took an extreme turn for the worse and became notoriously violent. The marijuana guys were mellow and assigned an almost union-like pay scale to each task. If you were a crewman on the Cigarette boat, you were paid $10,000. If you unloaded the boat, you were paid $1,500. If you drove the truck that transported the pot from the house to the warehouse, you were paid an additional $1,000. It was a business, and it made sense that everyone, at every level, feel like they were being treated fairly.

We needed at least $5,000 to rent an apartment for three months in Manhattan, which would amount to one night of work unloading a Cigarette boat packed with marijuana. I know this sounds like one of those, "This one time at band camp…," shocker stories, and it is. That is how some, and I won't say which, members of The Spinouts raised enough money to get to NYC. We were hired to unload a boat stuffed with marijuana and carry it into a nice waterfront house on Bay Drive in chic Surfside. Dressed in black pants and shirts, that's what we did.

When the capacious Cigarette boat pulled up to the back of the house at around 1:30 a.m., a crewman opened the hatch of the boat and started tossing bales of marijuana onto the dock. The

New York City

moon was almost full that evening, which meant that we were in plain sight of probably no less than five houses on the other side of the narrow strip of Biscayne Bay that separated the homes. In the bright light, it felt like what we were doing was nuts. Screw it, this was not the time for second-guessing. With my adrenaline pumping and my heart racing, I grabbed the first bale and carried it to the next guy that stood between the dock and the house. He in turn handed it to another guy, who carried it into the house. This procedure repeated itself for approximately 25 minutes. 25 incredibly long minutes! With all of the marijuana bales inside the house, the two crew members brought the roaring engines of the boat to life and slipped away, as if they had never been there at all.

I'd like to be able to tell you that I was cool and calm while the bales were being counted, but I can't; I was terrified. There was an entire room filled with marijuana. It wasn't an ounce, or a pound, **it was one hundred, 40-pound bales!** I anticipated that at any moment, armed DEA agents would come bursting through the front door and haul us all off to jail. The money it would cost in lawyers and fines, and the legal trouble that I would be in, would not be worth the $1,500 that I was making that night. What had I been thinking?

The 100 bales of marijuana were finally all re-counted and stacked neatly in the room, and 30 minutes later we were given the go ahead to leave the house. We all got in the car that we had arrived in, and five minutes later, relatively sure we weren't going to get busted, we started giggling like little girls and continued on to The Ham and Eggery in North Miami Beach for corned beef hash and sunny-side up eggs. The next week we were each paid $2,000 cash. I remember being happy that we were paid a little extra money for our work, but also thinking what a complete fucking idiot I was for doing it in the first place.

New York City

The fact is, had we not done it, we would never have made it out of South Florida, and my life would be radically different today.

It was all in the name of fame!

It was September of 1983, and I immediately started making plans to go to New York City. The idea was for me to go up by myself, find us a place to live for three months, and book as many shows as possible. The guys agreed to it, and Steve and George each gave me $1,500 in cash to rent an apartment. Jack would be staying with a relative in Brooklyn, so he didn't chip in any money.

Sometimes a little ignorance works to one's advantage because the plan, although simple to devise, would need a lot of things to go remarkably right. I had never been to any big city, much less New York City, so I had no idea what to expect. I naively pictured New York to be like Florida, easy to find an affordable place to live and easy to book shows if you were a decent original band. Of course, New York is nothing like Florida.

We had no idea what an apartment would end up costing, so I needed to conserve as much cash as possible. Amtrak was running a weekday special: $50 one-way to any city. Therefore, train was the most economical way to travel. For the trip, I had on a pair of faded, ripped, Levi blue jeans, a random T-shirt, and beat-up, black Converse sneakers. Inside of my cheap, vinyl, Pan Am duffel bag was a plain grey sweatshirt and a few extra boxer underwear, tube socks, and T-shirts. Not much more than that. I double-checked that my pants pockets didn't have holes in them because that's where I stuffed all the cash.

When I reached Penn Station in New York City, I would locate the #2 subway train and ride it to the last stop, Flatbush Avenue.

New York City

From there, I would walk to my cousin Sophie's house on Avenue K and 33rd Street. That's where I would establish a temporary "base camp" to figure out my next move. Sophie had graciously offered to let me stay at her place as long as I needed and had given me the simple instructions to get to her house from Penn Station. Near the end of our conversation, she also advised me to refer to the subway train as the "train" not the "subway" so I wouldn't appear to be from out of town.

Twenty-eight hours after stepping onto the Amtrak at the Hollywood Boulevard station in Florida, the train doors opened, and I was finally in New York City. I was very excited, but I was also a bit cautious. I had heard about how dangerous New York was and I had a lot of cash on me. I wasn't going to let anybody know I was a newbie, so I followed the signs and walked confidently and purposefully towards the #2 train. Along the way, I picked up *The Village Voice* so that I could get a list of clubs that hired live bands. I enjoyed the 40-minute subway ride from Penn Station to Flatbush Avenue, taking in and enjoying this new experience. I was already feeling the energy of NYC.

Sophie's house was a small, typical Brooklyn duplex, and it felt nice to be there. The last few months, I had focused much more on The Spinouts than on my college courses. The result was that I had failed two courses. I had intended to drop both courses early on but didn't realize that there was paperwork that had to be turned in, so henceforth, two F's appeared on my permanent record. I had placed a tremendous amount of pressure on myself to help the band succeed, so at this point, I just needed a little "normal" in my life. Sophie had two, young 8 and 10-year-old sons, Mark and Sam, and it was fun to just hang out with them and be a part of the family.

New York City

Of course, I was there to do a job, and for that, Sophie's brother, Murray, had volunteered to come over to help me get oriented. Right after the nice family dinner, Murray and I got busy. My plan was to knock on the door of every club that booked live original bands and present our record, picture, and cassette demo tape, so that we could be put on the schedule to play. Our system was simple. Murray marked on the subway map the addresses of the clubs listed in *The Village Voice* that I wanted to visit, and then showed me which trains would get me there. By marking every one of the clubs on the map, depending on who was available at what times and on which days, I would be able to plan the most efficient manner to get there. In theory, that was the idea. In practice, it was a cluster fuck. I spent the next four days lost and wearing down my Chuck Taylors to the nubs.

Without Murray's help, I wouldn't even have known where to begin. When we were done with the logistics, Sophie, Sam, and Mark came into the living room and filled me in on life in the big city. Then, it was time to play-wrestle with the boys again. I was in a good place mentally and was ready for Manhattan.

The next morning, Tuesday, at around 11 a.m., I called each of the clubs to inquire when I could come by. By one o'clock, I had stepped off the #5 train at Broadway and Lafayette and was now in Manhattan. I needed to get to Greenwich Village, which according to the subway map, would be relatively close. I began to walk. I walked, and walked, and walked some more. At first, the walking didn't bother me because I was excited to be in Manhattan, and having lived in hot, humid Florida my whole life, had never experienced weather as lovely as this. It was 60 degrees with no humidity, and the sun was shining through a clear blue sky. By 4:30 however, I had zigzagged from north to south and from east to west and had only been to three clubs. I was starting to drag a little bit. It occurred to me that the small

New York City

distances on the subway map equated to large distances by foot (duh). I only had $10 per day budgeted for expenses, so my legs inevitably remained the dominant means of transportation. Obviously, I needed a better plan and a little help from friends.

So, I called upon my ex-girlfriend Sonnie, who had moved to New York six months ago with her bestie, Rose, and met them both at my friend Alex Mitchel's apartment on Suffolk Street. Alex was one of the first from the South Florida music scene to move up to New York and he shared an apartment with his guitar player, Mario Sorrentino (Skippy). In Florida, Alex and Skippy had fronted a band called The Throbs, which was an entry-level punk band. After The Throbs disbanded, Alex and Skippy formed a band called Crucial Truth, which surprisingly, did not sound anything at all like The Throbs. The first time I heard them, I did a double take. These guys were the real deal. They were a powerful, NYC style hardcore band. It was the first time I acknowledged Alex as a true lead singer and frontman. A year later, in 1984, Isaac Baruch finally heeded my advice to replace himself as lead singer of The U.S. Furys, by bringing in Alex. The new band was called St. Mary's Children of Salvation and Alex Mitchel was the singer, Ricky "Beck" Mahler was the bass player, Isaac played guitar, and the drummer was the brilliant Mark Evans, who was both very technical and tasteful. The band was superb and easily had the potential for top of the charts type of success, but they broke up when Isaac moved to Los Angeles. St. Mary's Children of Salvation was the precursor to Circus of Power, which formed in 1986 with me as drummer.

After yet another formidable walk from the Village, I managed to get to Alex and Skippy's apartment by around 6 p.m., and we were joined there by Sonnie and Rose. I had walked non-stop for five hours and had met with only two Greenwich Village club booking agents. The third club I went to that day, nobody even

New York City

answered the door. It was not a very productive day, so it was comforting to now be hanging out with my good friends from South Florida. Sonnie and I had been on and off again as boyfriend and girlfriend for years. Regardless of our official relationship status, we always remained good friends.

Sonnie knew that I needed to rent an apartment and informed me of how difficult that was. The only way to find an apartment, she advised, was to wake up very early on Wednesday, the day *The Village Voice* came out, and pick one up as soon as it got dropped off at the newspaper stand. She warned that by 10 a.m. there already would be a mob of people at every available apartment. People in NYC even combed the obituaries to try and snag rent stabilized apartments from the families of the deceased. This seemed insane to me, but I believed her, and so picked up the *Voice* early the next morning. I was a little late getting to the first apartment, which was in the East Village on 7th Street and 2nd Avenue, and sure enough, by 10 a.m. there were ten prospective renters in the apartment and somebody was already in the process of signing a rental contract. Scary.

I got to the next apartment, in the West Village on 10th Street between West 4th Street and Bleecker Street, by around 11 a.m. It was a hip-looking area of gorgeous tree-lined streets. Without knowing anything about NYC's neighborhoods, I immediately thought to myself that I would enjoy living here. Unbeknownst to me, the West Village was predominantly gay, and the two guys in charge of renting the apartment perked up when I walked into their office. I may not have known that the neighborhood was gay, but it was obvious that these middle-aged guys were, and based on the way they were fawning over me, could tell that they definitely liked what they saw! I was wearing the same ripped blue jeans that lived on my body and a plain, tight T-shirt. I played the part of the naive young boy from

New York City

Florida that needed to rent an apartment in the big city... "Would they rent it to me? Please?? Pretty please??? Oh gosh, I dropped my pen!" That's right, I worked it bitch! Going to see the apartment, which was a two-bedroom railroad flat, was just a technicality. I couldn't believe my good luck. They wanted a security deposit, but when I explained to them that all I had was $4,500 total and was willing to pay it all upfront, they made a light-hearted comment about "trusting me" and giggled as they accepted the $4,500 in cash for the three months of rent. It wasn't cheap, but it definitely was not above the market rate, and they could have easily rented that apartment for even more. We signed the contract and they gave me the keys.

I went back to Alex's house to call some more clubs. One of the clubs that I was hoping to book was CBGB. I called, and the man who answered told me to stop in anytime that afternoon between 5 and 6 p.m. The man on the phone turned out to be none other than Hilly Kristal, one of the biggest supporters on the face of the earth of live, original rock and roll. At 5 p.m. I got to CBGB, which thankfully was less than a 15-minute walk from Alex's apartment, and walked right into the dark bar. A Tommy Chong looking bearded man (Hilly) gruffly told me that they were closed, but when I told him that I had called and been told to bring over my cassette tape, his whole demeanor changed, and he enthusiastically welcomed me in. I showed him the record album and told him we were a psychobilly band from Florida and that we would be in NYC from October to January. He grabbed the cassette tape from my hand and listened to maybe 15 seconds of the first song and said, "Ok. I can book you on a Monday or a Tuesday night, and if you are any good and people come see you, I'll move you to a Wednesday the next time." He then took out his calendar and asked me if the first Monday in October would be okay. My insides were screaming, "Oh my God, The Spinouts are booked at CBGB!" I said, "Thank

New York City

you," and that we would see him then. The whole exchange took less than five minutes. It was only a start, but a really good one. If we could have chosen only one place to play, it would have been CBGB. My appreciation, and admiration of Hilly Kristal started that day and continued to grow as the scope of what this man was doing and accomplishing began to dawn on me more and more as time passed by. There are not too many people that had a bigger effect on the world of original live music than Hilly Kristal. By keeping CBGB open, instead of selling the valuable real estate that the club stood on, he provided an outlet for thousands of original bands to play their music. Some of those bands that got their start at CBGB became mega stars. Unfortunately, people like Hilly, who passed away in 2007, just don't come around too often, and he will be impossible to replace. Sickeningly, a John Varvatos boutique now stands where CBGB used to be.

The next two days, I was able to lock in October shows at Great Gildersleeves, which was a large club in the Bowery where many cool bands such as Iggy Pop, Elvis Costello, and J. Geils Band played at when they were first coming up, and at Kenny's Castaways. Pat Kenny, of Kenny's Castaways, was very enthusiastic about booking The Spinouts and I got a great, genuine vibe from him. Kenny's Castaways was a known hangout of record company executives and A&R people. We were also booked at The Other End on Bleecker Street. I dealt directly with Paul Colby, who made me feel as if The Spinouts were a mega band. The Other End, now known as The Bitter End, has hosted a who's who of the rock elite. Bob Dylan, Van Morrison, Stevie Wonder, and so many other legends of the entertainment world had been hired by the same Paul Colby to play there. Hilly, Pat, and Paul were the wizards behind the curtain of the NYC music scene, and they treated me, an absolute nobody with a yet unproven, most-likely second-rate

New York City

band, with all the courtesy due the manager of an established mega band. Surly there is some lesson to be learned from that. To round out our schedule, we were also booked at RT Firefly at 75 Bleecker, where Cheetah Chrome had done a show only a year earlier, and WGAF on E. 2nd Avenue and 12th Street. Armed with nothing but persistence and *The Village Voice*, combined with a little luck, my one-week trip to NYC was a great success. Steve, George, and I had a lovely apartment to stay at and the band was booked to play six shows in October. It was a job well done and would make for a great start for us.

I thanked Alex and Skippy for letting me hang out at their place, Sonnie and Rose for their street-smarts advice, and my cousins Sophie and Murray for taking me in and helping me, no questions asked. On Monday, eight days after I had first arrived in NYC, I got back on the Amtrak train at Penn Station and headed back to Florida.

Between the money I had just put up for rent in NYC and the expenses that I had incurred during the trip, I was flat broke again. The three band members each reimbursed me $75, which was the fair thing to do, and I didn't have much more than that in my pocket for our voyage back to New York 10 days later. I mention how much money I had because most people would probably think it irresponsible, or even crazy, to travel 1,500 miles to a new city with access to only a couple of hundred dollars total…no ATM back-up, no credit card, no nothing. Neither of us, again except Steve, had access to any money at all, except what was in our pockets. In order to survive the three months in NYC, we would need to find jobs, and find them fast.

The problem was that in 1983, the United States was just clawing its way out of the worst recession since the early 70's. As a matter of fact, unemployment had reached the highest level

New York City

since the great depression. Translation: we weren't getting jobs anytime soon. But we didn't know that. We didn't even know what the word recession meant. We were about to find out, firsthand, what a recession really was.

Stayin' Alive in NYC

The following Friday morning, we loaded the amplifiers, guitars, and drum set into the 1975 Ford Econoline van that Steve had bought for $1,100 and departed for the West Village in NYC. The trip went smoothly and we arrived on a gorgeous, cool, Saturday afternoon. Our apartment was a one-floor walk-up, which made it a pain to carry the amplifiers and drums up the stairs. Jack Stone didn't even bother to help with the equipment. As soon as we arrived, he took off to go wherever he was staying at in Brooklyn. Was this a sign of things to come?

There was really nothing to do or take care of before our Monday gig at CBGB, so we just walked around the West Village and relaxed at the apartment. Of course, I immediately bought *The Village Voice* at the newsstand on 7th Avenue and Christopher Street. There it was: **Monday Night CBGB - The Spinouts**. I know it was only a Monday, but it was CBGB. I had dreamed of playing at CBGB since I was 17 years old. The Reactions had listened to the record *Loud, Fast, Rules* by The Stimulators, which featured a young kid named Harley Flanagan on the drums, and we immediately wanted to do a gig at CBGB with Harley's band. When I finally met Harley in 1984, I was brand new to the intimidating Sunday Hardcore Matinee scene, and Harley always made sure nothing bad happened to me there. Harley eventually founded the internationally acclaimed Cro-Mags, whose debut album, *Age of Quarrel*, often described as a seminal album, actually didn't even do the band justice. The magnitude and power of Cro-Mags had to be experienced live in order to be fully appreciated. In 1986, after Harley switched from

Stayin' Alive in NYC

bass to drums, he asked me to join the Cro-Mags and go on tour with him. I reluctantly declined because I was enrolled at Baruch College and needed to be in NYC when the semester began. I wanted to play with Harley and the Cro-Mags so badly! Since I couldn't, Petey Hines, the young, powerful drummer from Murphy's Law took the spot, and was a perfect fit for them.

Monday arrived, and The Spinouts were scheduled to go onstage at 10 p.m. We weren't headlining, but at least we didn't have to go on at 9 p.m. when CBGB was completely empty. As soon as we broke into the first song, which was a high-energy, rockabilly-like instrumental, we were all immediately reminded of what we were there to do. We were there to rock the house! There were only 15 or 20 people total in the bar, but we gave it our all as if it was Madison Square Garden. Playing music was what we loved to do and what drove us to do all the things that we had done to get here. We knew it was going to be a long road and were happy just to be on it. I called Hilly later that week and he told me that he had liked what he had heard and acknowledged that there were at least a few people there to see us, so he was willing to book us for a Wednesday evening at the beginning of November. Sounded good to me. That became the pattern at all the bars we played at. We would put on a good show to a relatively small audience and then get booked again for a better night and a better time slot. In drips and drabs, more and more people came to see us each time. Drips and drabs was all we were realistically expecting because it takes time for people to hear about a band. It's a process. That's the reason bands have to stay together for many years in order to get discovered. They must allow the process to play out. We were going to be in NYC for only three months, so we were hoping to be discovered by the record industry, before the public had actually discovered us yet. New York City was the right place for that to happen.

Stayin' Alive in NYC

George and I had been searching the Help Wanted section of the newspaper with no luck. The weather was getting colder and our pockets were getting threadbare. The money that we received from playing at clubs was based on how much was collected at the door and then divided among the bands that had played that evening. It didn't amount to much, ranging from $35 to $125, and then that was divided among the four band members. Receiving any money at all meant that we could eat for a few more days, but gig money was obviously not the solution. It was becoming urgent that we find paying jobs. Steve Lambert, who had money and could have ate sushi everyday if he wanted to, was willing to live in the same exact conditions as George and I, and pitch in financially only what George and I were pitching in. Neither George nor I ever even considered asking Steve to pitch in more than us and appreciated and respected that Steve willingly sacrificed his lifestyle so we would all deal with the same circumstances as a team, a family, a band, and not as individuals. At one point towards the end of October, we pooled our money and bought a 20 lb. sack of brown rice for around $8. For weeks after, each night, I would buy literally less than two dollars worth of fresh tofu and vegetables, combine it with the brown rice, and that's what the three of us would have for dinner. The tofu that was available in the Korean markets came in two sizes: the small was 25 cents and the large was 35 cents. It was so fresh that you literally plucked it out of the water with tongs. Tofu contains a lot of protein and, in my opinion, was the best food value for the money at the time. I credit tofu as the biggest reason we didn't starve to death that winter. We also had cans of tuna, peanut butter, and boxes of Kraft Mac 'n' Cheese in our pantry for variety. In spite of those tough circumstances, there was never any bickering among us, and even though alcohol was not in our budget, we managed to always enjoy ourselves.

Stayin' Alive in NYC

In spite of the radically frugal way we were stretching our very limited dollars, we were reaching the point where there might not be anything left to stretch out. The three of us had lost a lot of weight, and we were all thin to begin with, so it was time for emergency measures. We couldn't wait any longer to find jobs, so early one morning, I set out with the intention of not coming home until I found a job. I walked to 6th Avenue, where there was plenty of restaurants, and then headed north. I stopped in at every restaurant on the west side of the avenue from 10th Street to 32nd Street and every restaurant on the east side of the avenue on the way back down to 4th Street. I must have visited 25 restaurants and nobody needed a single waiter? This seemed insane to me! After a few hours, I was even asking if a busboy position was open. Most restaurants told me that they weren't even accepting new applications because they already had a waiting list, while a few others had me leave my contact information. I got back to West 4th Street as it was starting to get dark out, and not only was I tired from the walking and rejection but was also a little flustered by how intense the restaurants had seemed. I'm now accustomed to the intensity of NYC and would not settle for anything less, but that day, I was still a Florida boy, and obviously needed to up my game a little. Tired and dejected, I started walking down West 4th Street to my apartment. Tomorrow would be another day. As I was walking, I passed right by a cute shop called Pink Pussycat Boutique, which had a sign on the window that read: **Salesperson needed, please inquire inside**. I walked in, and after quickly identifying the most authoritative looking figure in the small shop, announced to him in a cheerful, enthusiastic voice, that he could put away the help wanted sign, because I would take the job. The authoritative looking man happened to be one of the (very gay) owners of Pink Pussycat Boutique, and he had loved what he heard and what he saw!

Stayin' Alive in NYC

"Oh my god," he said. "I **love** your confidence! Have you ever been a salesman before?" I thought about it for a moment, then rationalized that selling quarter ounce bags of weed did indeed qualify as a salesman job. "Yes, I have worked as a salesman before," I answered him honestly, "I live only a few blocks from here, and I would love to work here."

He gave me some tough talk about the requirements of the job and told me that the pay was $6.85 per hour, which was well above minimum wage, and then asked me when I could start.

It had happened so quickly and so unexpectedly, and I was so relieved to have found a job, that my head was spinning! I said thank you, and that I would be there the next morning. I was so excited to have found a job. It meant that I wasn't going to starve to death. I was only slightly concerned that I knew nothing about sex toys, which is what they sold at the Pink Pussycat Boutique. How hard, I mean how difficult, could it be?

The month of October was not very glamorous. We did our best to put on good shows at the clubs we were playing at in NYC, and that in itself was exciting, but we were playing to fewer people than we had played to in Florida. That little piece of information could have offered up a clue to unraveling what the future held in store for us. One of the better entertainment writers in South Florida once wrote in reference to The Reactions, "They will probably never pack The Agora (in Florida), even if they could fill The Garden (in NYC)," meaning South Florida audiences may never "get" The Reactions, but a more sophisticated and hipper NYC audience probably would. Maybe The Spinouts were the opposite, hot stuff in Miami, but lukewarm in NYC? It also felt gloomy to be broke and have to think about how we were spending every measly cent.

Stayin' Alive in NYC

To put our financial predicament into perspective, at one of our shows, Jack had met three girls who indicated that they wanted to hang out with the band at our apartment sometime. A few nights later, the girls and Jack came over at around 9 p.m., long after Steve and I had finished our de-rigueur tofu, sprouts, vegetables, and brown rice dinner. The girls were all good-looking, in their early to mid-twenties, and were there for just one purpose; to fuck the band. It had been a while, so we were not opposed to that. The three girls brought over an assortment of falafels and gyros to eat at our apartment and were sitting on the couch enjoying their dinner while we made small talk. Neither Steve nor I were looking at the girls. We were looking at the food! We were fucking salivating and would have handily chosen the food over the girls. Somewhere along the line, the girls figured it out and offered us the food. Not to share the food with us, but actually offered us all the food to eat. Steve and I didn't hesitate. We inhaled the Mediterranean delicacies. This was probably not the first time these girls had been around a starving band before, because they didn't skip a beat, but rather, offered to go downstairs and buy some beers. These girls were a godsend. When the food was all consumed and we were now relaxed and enjoying the beers, we finally focused our attention on the girls themselves. I zeroed in on one really cute girl that looked like one of those chic women's clothing boutique sales girls that guys always want to bang when they go shopping with their wives or girlfriends. That's how they get you to stay in the store and buy clothes. They tease you just enough so you'll buy the clothes. Works every time. Jack and Steve left the apartment with two of the girls to go to a club, and I got to stay behind and bang the sales girl. During our feverish romp, I tied her wrists up to the shower curtain rod. The next morning, right before she left for work (she really did work at a women's clothing boutique nearby in the Village!), she asked if she could repay the

Stayin' Alive in NYC

favor by tying me up to a chair. I barely even knew this girl's first name, so of course I responded, "Sure, why not!" She tied me up so I couldn't escape and proceeded to have some pretty hot sex with me. Right after, while I was still naked and tied up, she started going through Steve's drawers, which was uncool because Steve was real touchy about anybody going through his stuff, till she found some scissors, and then walked over to me. With an evil, twisted look on her face, she let me know that she could kill me if she wanted to. For a moment, I was kind of second-guessing my decision to allow her to tie me up. Maybe I hadn't thought it all the way through? Then she laughed, thanked me for a fun time, got dressed and left the apartment. It took five minutes after she was gone to escape from the chair.

October was gloomy, but obviously not a complete washout. I finally had a job, and in a few days, George would also get a job arranging and delivering flowers at a shop on Hudson Street. I was selling marital sex aids and George was working in a gay flower shop. Who would have ever imagined?

My job at the Pink Pussycat was quite the adventure for a 21-year-old with only moderate sex experience. I had never even seen a vibrator or dildo in person before taking the job at the Pink Pussycat. Turned out I was a natural, because for the two months I worked there, I sold lots of Ben Wa balls, whips and restraints, and many different types of dildos and vibrators, including one that had a truly ingenious rotating and vibrating clitoral stimulator attached. Looked like fun! Our biggest seller in the gay West Village was amyl-nitrate (poppers), which apparently prolongs and intensifies the orgasm of a guy. I once even helped a gorgeous, very well-dressed, high-class escort pick out a leather strap-on dildo and some other toys, to use on the totally submissive, nerdy client following her around the entire store like a puppy dog. When it was time to pay, she

Stayin' Alive in NYC

ordered him to hand over his American Express Gold Card to me. I enjoyed being a part of that kinkiness.

My most memorable transaction was to Steven Tyler of Aerosmith, who had come to the shop with his wife after a New York Dolls reunion show in the Village. I had always imagined him to be a cool, nice guy, and after meeting him that night, my pre-conceived notion of him was confirmed. He came in dressed as the rock god that he is, wearing his trademark scarves draped around his neck. I immediately said hello and asked him what he was doing in the area. You know, a normal question to ask Steven Tyler who has wandered into a sex toys boutique with his wife. The other salesman working that night, who also like me was a struggling musician from out of town, asked me if that was Steve Tyler. I told him it was definitely Steve Tyler, but that wasn't enough for this guy. The blond-haired salesman from Minneapolis, Minnesota then walks up to Steven Tyler, and asks him if he really is Steven Tyler! I was so embarrassed that I wanted to disappear. Steven handled it well. He smiled and said yes, that he was indeed, Steven Tyler. That was **still** not enough to convince the salesman, so he further asked, "If you're really Steven Tyler, then what song did you open with at your concert in Minneapolis last year?" Steve Tyler not only answered it correctly, but then also proceeded to show his driver's license ID. As a way of apologizing to Mr. Tyler for the uncalled-for interrogation, I charged him for only half of the stuff he purchased. As he was leaving the shop, he was even affable enough to tell us which hotel he was staying at and invited us both to come hang out with him. Turned out that the job at the Pink Pussycat Boutique was infinitely more interesting than the waiter job I had gone seeking.

What really changed for me in November was that I started to venture to the dirty, dangerous, east side of the Village, where

Stayin' Alive in NYC

the real music scene was happening. Now that I didn't have to worry about starving, I started hanging out with my buddies from the band St. Mary's Children of Salvation, Ricky, Alex, and Isaac, to check out the other rock and roll bands that were playing around town. We saw a lot of different bands, but what really impressed me was how good the punk and hardcore bands were. At first, I was going to CBGB a few times a week to see the "regular" rock bands, but then I started going more and more only to see the punk and hardcore shows, especially the Sunday Hardcore Matinee. After watching these new and exciting bands play, I began to doubt whether The Spinouts really had what it took to succeed in NYC.

At the hardcore shows, I usually hung out with Sonnie, Gina, and Johnny Stiff. Johnny Stiff was the booking agent for any and all punk and hardcore bands that played on the East Coast. He knew every music promoter from Baltimore to Boston. If you wanted to play on the Northeast Corridor, Johnny was the man to book it for you. Sonnie had moved in with her good friend from the Miami punk scene, Gina Zayas, who was Johnny Stiff's girlfriend. Gina went on to help form the fierce, all-girl band Pre Metal Syndrome (PMS) with her sister, and my good friend and fellow drummer, Carmen Marrero, lead guitar player Liz Brockland, who was the girlfriend of the phenomenal bass player Zowie, who would eventually join Circus of Power, and Ally Gamble on bass. The lead singer of PMS, Yana Chupenko, with her gorgeous Ukrainian face and booming, flawless voice, was destined to be in the limelight. When I first started attending classes at Baruch College, Yana would ask me how I was able to make it through school with all of the craziness going on around us. I told her that it was worth it, and that with only a little effort could be accomplished by anyone. Soon after, she also signed up for classes at Baruch, and I was happy and proud when Yana went on to graduate with a Bachelor's degree. I wished that

Stayin' Alive in NYC

every young person in the Lower East Side could go to school so that one day they could all live better lives. It's one thing to be a street kid at age 22 (which I was), but at 32, or 42, it really sucks.

Knowing and being friends with Johnny Stiff and Sonnie went a long way to helping me fit in with the wild and sometimes violent downtown scene. I was not new to punk and hardcore, but the intensity of the NYC scene and the quality of the music was unlike anything I had ever envisioned. The Reactions would have loved this place! Even though Johnny Stiff hated mainstream music of any sort, Sonnie dragged him to Spinout shows so he could at least hear me play drums. Johnny thought I was wasting my talents with The Spinouts. I would laugh and tell him that I enjoyed playing with The Spinouts, and that I certainly was not wasting my time, or talents.

By the end of November, the thermometer had dipped into the 20's, and by December, the lows were in the teens. Trust me, global warming wasn't on anybody's radar yet. I invested in some thermal underwear from an army surplus store, a cheap $8 jacket from a thrift shop on the Brooklyn side of the Brooklyn Bridge, and some cheap gloves and a scarf from Chinatown, so I was in good shape. The Spinouts however, were beginning to "spin out." We were playing live shows once a week but hadn't practiced once since the end of September, and it was starting to show. This was New York. You had to be sharp at every single gig and you had to give it your all at every single performance. You just never knew when you were going to be discovered.

None of us in the band ever had anything against Jack. He was a little different, maybe a little close-minded, but we all liked him. Unfortunately, maybe as a result of living on his own, he became completely disengaged from the rest of the band. Steve, George, and I were willing to keep an open mind and continue

Stayin' Alive in NYC

progressing and getting better. Jack was stuck on his narrow views and hated anything to do with change, including probably New York City itself. The final time that we played at Great Gildersleeves, Jack kept his back to the audience the entire show. I had no interest in taking on Jack as a long-term head-case project, so after the show, I quit the band. George and Steve seemed relieved by my decision, and we made it official. The Spinouts were done. We played our final show on December 7th, ironically at CBGB, and two nights after, on Friday, December 9th, we were back in the 1975 Ford Econoline van heading back towards South Florida.

The Slums of South Beach

This was a tough pill to swallow. I understand that we all need to pay our dues, but this was fucking brutal. I hadn't given any thought to what I would be doing when we were done in New York, but this certainly wasn't what I had in mind. I had stayed in a killer apartment in the West Village of NYC, played at CBGB three times in two months, and had seen some of the finest bands in the nation on a weekly basis. I had managed not to starve or freeze to death, fucked my fantasy sales girl, and had sold a 12-inch dildo to Steven Tyler. How does one go from Steven Tyler, of fucking Aerosmith, back to the same bedroom that I had been in since fourth grade? Every cell of my mind and body wanted to scream "Noooooo!"

It was really strange to also be back in my parents' house in North Bay Village. Fortunately, I didn't have to wallow in my own pool of depressing self-pity for too long. Within a few days I was rescued when the opportunity presented itself to join the uber-cool, ultra-notorious band, Crank. I know those types of descriptions are easily thrown around when describing a local band, especially after five shots of tequila, when the band becomes soooo awesome, but Crank was world-class cool. They would have been huge in Berlin or in Los Angeles. I **loved** Crank, and was good friends with the departing drummer, Johnny Sticks, who was moving back to North Carolina to tend to some family issues. I also knew that everybody in the band, except the straight-laced, ridiculously talented bass player, Larry Lee, was a full-blown junkie. That did not concern me too much though. I wanted the full rock and roll experience, and what's

The Slums of South Beach

more rock and roll than jabbing needles filled with heroin and cocaine into your veins? Crank was Elaine, Johnny Salton, Billy Weasel, and from Portland, Oregon, Larry Lee. We rehearsed at Elaine's art studio loft on Michigan Avenue, right on Lincoln Road. Do you have any idea what rent for a storefront on South Beach's Lincoln Road goes for today? Probably around $20k per month. But in December of 1983, when South Beach was a slum, Elaine rented her storefront loft for $260 per month. That's where Crank rehearsed, and of course, shot up drugs. Before rehearsal, I would have to drive Johnny, Elaine, and Billy, in the faded red Dodge Dart that my Tia Matilde had sold me for $300, to Overtown so they could buy their drugs. Overtown is where the housing projects are in Miami, and I would wait parked in the street where I could see the gang members with their gold teeth and drawn guns. Johnny told me not to worry…they would never shoot me because that would be bad for business. I knew it didn't necessarily work that way. If they shot me dead that night, just as many people would be there to score drugs the following night. What choice would they have? But I wasn't overly concerned, I understood the point Johnny was trying to make. Murder was probably bad for business. The Spinouts were a Disney World band of preppy pretty boys compared to Crank. I had no illusions of relying on Crank for my future, but in my heart, I knew that a band like Crank was a better fit for me than the squeaky-clean Spinouts. Johnny Stiff had been correct.

As soon as my new bandmates were back in the car, they immediately went about their business of tying off and injecting themselves with the narcotics. Ten minutes later, by the time we had crossed the Julia Tuttle Causeway onto Miami Beach, all three were flying high, and we were ready to rehearse. This was our nightly routine in preparation for a big, Saturday, December 24th gig at Flynn's on 71st Street and Collins Avenue on Miami Beach. It had been a long time since I had hung out with my

The Slums of South Beach

Reactions brother, Johnny Salton. Johnny had changed quite a bit. Rather than smoking pot every day, he had graduated to shooting heroin, but his encyclopedic knowledge of bands from around the world remained. How did he keep so up-to-date on what was happening in California and in London? Miami was so isolated from anything that was new or cutting-edge. While we were messing around at rehearsal one night, right before a rest break, we started playing "Ace of Spades" by Motörhead. A quarter of the way through the song, I sped the tempo up so that we were now playing it "hardcore" style. When we finished, Johnny, who often shared his interesting nuggets of random musical information with me, told me of a band from California called Battalion of Saints that played a killer version of "Ace of Spades." I nodded his way and said, "Cool." I had never heard of Battalion of Saints. How could I have? Within eight months of that rehearsal, I was the new drummer of Battalion of Saints.

What were the odds of that?

I needed only eight credits at MDCC to obtain my AA degree, and I could see the finish line. From January 1984 until I graduated on May 26th, 1984, I went to school and got good grades during the day, and at night descended into the world that was Crank. My lifestyle was so much different than the other members of Crank. I exercised and went to school everyday and at rehearsals drank alcohol, if anything, while everybody else except Larry was high on dope and coke.

The Christmas Eve show at Flynn's was memorable. Johnny, Billy, and Elaine got to the club preposterously late and **absurdly** high. Crank had always been a popular band in South Florida, so the place was packed. Elaine was an oxymoron; a junkie with a smoking body. She taught a yoga class during the day and her thin, 5'9" frame was cut with the sinuous, sexy

The Slums of South Beach

dancer muscle of a tall, dark-haired sex goddess, and that night she was dressed only in body paint for the show. The stingiest triangle of a G-string covered her vagina and everything else, body paint. Elaine seemed to be as high as a person can possibly be without OD'ing, as were Johnny and Billy, and was going to play the sold-out club almost naked. I fucking loved this!

Crank was Velvet Underground, Joy Division, Iggy Pop, and good old-fashioned American hardcore wrapped up into one dark, sloppy, edgy, and very opiated band. Elaine was sexy, even sexual, in a writhing, dark haired Marianne Faithfull meets Patti Smith sort of way, and fronted a band that was not afraid to push the limits of what music was **supposed** to be. Like Elaine, this band was also an oxymoron, both dark and energetic, at the same time. We started the set with "Endless Sky," the B-side of their fabulous studio recording, *Breaking the Law*. My favorite line from the song is, "I can't get no relief from R O L A I D S," an obvious reference to heroin. We continued with a one-and-a-half hour set of mostly originals. It was a killer show, but when we were done, there were no encores. Elaine, Billy, and Johnny immediately disappeared from the club à la Johnny Thunders. I saw Johnny Thunders play at Irving Plaza in NYC only a few years before he died of a heroin overdose. I was close enough to see him puke during his set from being so ludicrously high. In rock and roll, there is a fine line between putting on a wonderfully sloppy rock and roll show and just being embarrassingly sloppy. Between being deliriously high and dying of an overdose. It's only a super fine line that separates life and death in rock and roll.

Truth be told, these were not very inspiring times in South Florida. The great bands of the early 80's were all mostly gone, and people seemed oddly content with the mediocrity that abounded, as if they were making the best with what they had to

The Slums of South Beach

work with. In addition, there was a real sliminess to all of South Florida, especially Miami Beach. If you can somehow picture it, South Beach in 1984 was a dirty, depressing, dangerous ghetto. I wasn't sure what my future held, but as soon as I graduated MDCC, my future would be somewhere other than in South Florida. I was still counting on fate to give me a sign as to exactly where that would be, and how I would get there.

Fate came to me in the form of a three-piece band called Menstrual Cycle. Sorry, that was the real name of the band. I was still playing in Crank, when a friend of mine from back in the day, a young man named Mario Von Shock contacted me in March with a proposal. Shock spun me a tale of how he had moved to London from Hialeah and become very popular as a musician and as a tattoo artist. The punk and hardcore scene in London was the real thing, so if he was telling me the truth, this would be a big deal, so I at least had to hear him out. Turns out, as unlikely as it seemed, he was telling the truth. He had moved in with Charlie Harper, the singer of the famous English punk band UK Subs, and had released his own record, ½ Skin ½ Punx, that had met with some moderate success. Menstrual Cycle had a few shows lined-up on the East Coast of the United States with Agnostic Front, and a gig opening up for the U.K. Subs at The Rock Hotel in NYC, and their drummer, Hippie, had quit the band. I customarily never endorsed tasteless, gimmicky names such as Menstrual Cycle, but screw it, I was up for a free ride back to New York City.

For the month of March, I rehearsed back at Sync Studios with Mario Von Shock and his bass player, Trash Compactor, or TC as he was called. Mario had a bit of a reputation as somewhat of a bullshit artist, and sometimes had trouble backing up all of his talk. But I really liked Mario. He was guilty only of flying too high, and I could never blame him for doing what he had to do

The Slums of South Beach

to get the fuck out of Hialeah, which is no place for a punk rocker with a free spirit. I also thought TC was a great guy, with a heart of gold. If you looked at either of them, with their large, spiked Mohawks, multiple piercings, tattoos, red suspenders, studded leather jackets, and hardcore boots, maybe you would describe them differently. But in my eyes, they were both just super nice kids, and because of how I felt about them, was going to help them on their tour. Normally, free trip to NYC or not, I wouldn't have played with inferior musicians, especially in a band with a name like Menstrual Cycle. Von Shock and TC were super stoked that I had joined them.

I had no idea how Menstrual Cycle would sound live. Some bands suck at rehearsal, but then kick ass during live shows, while other bands are great in the studio, but can't generate any excitement live. To find out where we stood, we booked two consecutive Saturday nights at Flynn's, with one of those nights, coincidentally, as the opening act for the visiting U.K. Subs. The two shows turned out better than I expected. We were tight, fast, loud, and energetic. One good thing about Von Shock and TC was that they looked the part of hardcore English punk rockers from head to toe. We were prepared and ready for our upcoming tour of the East Coast.

On Thursday, April 26th, 1984, I officially graduated with an Associate in Arts degree. There was no longer anything to tether me down or to hold me back. It was time to focus exclusively on Plan A, which was to become a rock star. Our short tour with the popular hardcore band, Agnostic Front, was to begin Saturday. In two days, I would be playing for the first time ever to a real East Coast hardcore audience in New Jersey, with engagements to follow in NYC, Philadelphia, Connecticut, and then back to NYC again. Friday afternoon arrived and I hopped on a plane to meet up with Von Shock and TC in NYC.

Finding Joey Wrecked

As soon as I got into the van at LaGuardia Airport with Roger Miret and Vinnie Stigma of Agnostic Front, I knew I wasn't in Kansas anymore. Holy fuck! Agnostic Front was the very top of the NYC hardcore music scene. They wore shaved heads and had tattoos up and down their arms and bodies. Roger even had his neck adorned with a startling tattoo of a spider web. I had never seen anything like them before, and if their goal was to scare the bejesus out of me, they nailed it. Johnny Stiff had asked them to pick me up at the airport, and it was incredibly magnanimous of them to do so.

They were both dressed sharply. Vinnie was wearing a band T-shirt, thin, red suspenders, and military-style fatigue pants tucked into his telltale skinhead, oxblood red Doc Maarten boots. An olive green Oi bomber jacket topped off his attire. Roger was wearing a black, Fred Perry polo shirt with a red emblem on it and Lee blue jeans with the cuffs rolled up over his DM's. Although they both looked like they unmistakably belonged onstage, this was more than just an image. This was who they really were. Clearly, they were committed, and just as clearly, there was no Plan B for these boys.

Being around Roger and Vinnie highlighted the fact that I was on the inside now and not just a curious, passive spectator on the outskirts of the crowd. This wasn't the gay West Village. This wasn't the mainstream world of mainstream music and mainstream people.

Finding Joey Wrecked

Agnostic Front was the epicenter of the violent, extreme world of early 1980's hardcore. They drove me to the corner of St. Marks place and 2nd Avenue, by the record store Free Being. I met up with Johnny Stiff, Sonnie, TC, Von Shock, and about 20 other hardcore locals. I took a moment to look around and gather it all in. This was where I wanted to be. This was what I wanted!

As relatively cool as I might have been by South Florida standards, Saint Marks Place was the heart of the NYC downtown scene, and I looked out of place. My appearance, my image, had always been important to me. When I was 17 and playing with The Reactions, I wore naturally ripped Levi jeans when nobody else wore ripped jeans, a T-shirt with the sleeves cut off and Converse sneakers. That was my "look," and it set me apart. With The Spinouts, I wore more formal clothes and pointy boots or Creepers, and again, it looked good on me and set me apart. But living in Miami Beach could not have possibly prepared me for the NYC hardcore scene. Since I was the new kid in town, the locals nevertheless treated me well and were willing to give me the opportunity to prove myself.

Our first show was an all-ages matinee at a VFW Hall in Long Branch, New Jersey. Agnostic Front went on stage first, and after just two songs I thought to myself, **"Why are these guys opening up for us?"** Agnostic Front was one of the most powerful bands I had ever heard in my entire life. The drummer and bass player were in absolute sync and were the foundation for an intense wall of sound from the guitars. Roger sang with a passion that made it difficult for the audience to not engage in. Menstrual Cycle, on the other hand, was a kind of flash in the pan band. It was clear to me that AF was in a totally different musical category. Nevertheless, our performance went off without a hitch. The next day in NYC, the Hardcore Matinee at CBGB was packed with skinheads and punks and I felt that I

Finding Joey Wrecked

was playing as if my life depended on it. The entire punk/hardcore scene was insanely intense. Although I wasn't nearby when it happened, Von Shock actually did end up getting punched in the face that day by a skinhead named Big Rob, who was upset that Mario had slept with a girlfriend of his named Jenny. These kids weren't dressing up to go and see a band play. These kids **were** punks, they **were** skinheads, 24/7, and many of them lived on the streets of the Lower East Side of New York City. I was from Miami Beach. I had a tan, enjoyed swimming at the beach. I had lot of toughening up to do.

The New London, Connecticut show went well on Friday night, but the show at Love Hall the following night in Philadelphia was marred by fight after fight between the punks and the skins. Without going too much into the history of punk, the traditional punk rock popularized by The Sex Pistols was now starting to be replaced by a more serious, more extreme form of punk called hardcore, whose supporters often had shaved heads and were called skinheads, or just skins, for short. Von Shock had created a degree of mystique by suggesting that punks and skins should get along and unite, but that union was starting to wear thin. Mario was able to calm things only temporarily as we played. The violent fighting continued the moment we got off the stage and stopped only after a wave of police officers rushed in to shut down the rest of the show.

Finally, on Sunday night we opened for U.K. Subs at Rock Hotel in NYC, and there were well over 1,000 hardcore punks and skins at the show. I played powerfully and energetically, and the crowd enjoyed our set. The U.K. Subs, however, were rock stars. They looked like rock stars, they moved and acted like rock stars, and they sounded like rock stars. That's how you needed to be to perform for thousands of people, instead of hundreds, and to sell hundreds of thousands of records, as opposed to 500.

Finding Joey Wrecked

The guitar player of The U.K. Subs that night was Captain Scarlet, who would eventually become the road manager of Battalion of Saints, and then when James Cooper was unceremoniously kicked out of the band, he became the new bass player as well. Scarlet and I became very good friends, and he stayed with me at my apartment in NYC until the day he left to go back to London. But that night, he was a rock star and I was the unknown drummer in the opening band.

According to Sonnie, I needed a makeover of my image. More bluntly, I needed to actually **find** an image. She was undoubtedly correct and was the perfect person to assist me. Sonnie, even while she was in Florida, had a high degree of fashion sense. She didn't spend a fortune on clothes and accessories but was always dressed uniquely and tastefully and always looked great. After only one year in NYC, she had taken her own look to a whole new level. In the timeless Woody Allen movie, *Hannah and Her Three Sisters*, there is a close-up of Sonnie sporting a glorious, multi-colored Mohawk during the punk rock scene, which was filmed at none other than CBGB. She was rocking a Mohawk way before Gwen Stefani!

From the moment that I landed in NYC, Sonnie had made it her mission to help me learn to dress better. I guess "dress for success" applies to more than just the business world. Finding one's image is not as easy as it sounds. It is a process, not an outfit or a costume. You have to become that person. To put it into Harry Potter terms, "The wizard doesn't choose their wand; it is the wand that chooses the wizard." You don't invent an image for yourself. It eventually just becomes who you are.

And so began the process of finding my image. I went way out of my comfort zone to try different pants, different shirts, different belts, different earrings and even different rings for my

Finding Joey Wrecked

fingers. Some worked and much of it didn't. After a short while, I could no longer even remember what I used to dress like, and what I used to look like. It was a total revamp, but most importantly, it fit with who I really was. Although it was springtime, I bought a well-made black leather motorcycle jacket down on Orchard Street at a good price, and a really cool punk rock studded leather belt. Not that phony crap that posers buy that are made in China, but rather, a well-made, quality leather belt. To round out my look, I replaced the Converse sneakers that I had been wearing since 6th grade with a pair of American made, black combat boots from an army surplus shop. It was great to have Sonnie around to make suggestions and to give me a thumb up or thumb down when needed, and I stayed with her working on my look for more than two weeks after the Menstrual Cycle gigs were over. Eventually, I needed to get back to Florida because I was still playing with Crank, and we had another show coming up in South Florida. Believe me, the Joey Wrecked that came back from New York looked nothing like the person that had one month ago left for NYC. I also didn't think the same or act the same. I had gotten a taste of my future and now I wanted to go live it. The disadvantage to looking the way I did was that I would no longer be able to get a job at a bank, not that I wanted a job at a bank anyway. There was no mistaking on what part of society I had landed on.

My days back in Florida were numbered anyway. I practiced with Crank and played one more show with them at Flynn's on July 12th. The band was nowhere near as stoned as the last time, and the music sounded much cleaner. It is very hard to properly tune a guitar when you are high on heroin, and at the previous show, Billy and Johnny had been very high indeed, and nowhere near in tune. Amazingly enough, the out of tune guitars hadn't ruined the show. This time, the guitars were tuned perfectly and it was completely different than our previous appearance. Not better, not worse, just different.

The following Sunday, the phone rang at my parents' house, and when I answered it, it was Johnny Stiff. He didn't say, "Hello," or, "How are you doing?" Johnny, in his thick Brooklyn accent said only, "You gotta come up ta New York right now!"

I considered it extremely odd that he was asking me to drop everything I was doing in order to immediately get on a plane to travel 1,500 miles, so I asked him what the F he was talking about. He just repeated, "You have to come up to New York today," but this time he added, "Battalion of Saints need a drummer to tour with." I got him to slow down and explain what was going on, but it was pretty straightforward. The drummer of the San Diego, California based Battalion of Saints decided to quit the band right before the start of a short, Northeast Coast tour. The band was now in NYC and in need of a drummer, and Johnny had recommended me.

"Okay," I calmly said. "Send me the airfare and I'll be on a plane on Monday morning." I was cool on the phone to Johnny, as if these sorts of offers were common, but holy crap, was this really happening? I had some minor things to take care of at home, but I was certainly going to take advantage of this random opportunity that had presented itself to me. Immediately after graduating MDCC I had left South Florida to play my first hardcore shows on the Northeast Coast. Now, exactly three months after opening for the U.K. Subs at The Rock Hotel, I was on the way back to NYC, and on the verge of joining the already well-known national band, Battalion of Saints. It had been an especially dark seven months, but I was finally back on track. Of course, I still had to pass my audition the following night.

Battalion of Saints

Let's be clear here, it wasn't fucking Mötley Crüe that I was auditioning for. Regardless, Battalion of Saints was a giant step up. In the era-defining punk rock book and movie, Steven Blush's *American Hardcore*, Battalion of Saints is mentioned as one of the top North American punk bands ever. In one of the scenes in the movie, Reed Mullin of Corrosion of Conformity appears in front of The Brewery in Raleigh, North Carolina and says, "We had **everybody**. We had Black Flag, Suicidal Tendencies, Cro-Mags, Battalion of Saints, and DOA." Mullin's Corrosion of Conformity is a very well-respected band that has stayed together for more than thirty years and sold hundreds of thousands of records. A musician of such stature speaking that way of Battalion of Saints is quite the compliment. Of the bands that he condenses down to as "everybody," Suicidal Tendencies was such an incredibly talented and creative band that they had their bass player scooped up by arguably one of the greatest bands ever, Metallica. Black Flag from Los Angeles and DOA from Vancouver were the pioneers of American punk rock and will be forever memorialized in our history books. And lastly, the Cro-Mags, who along with Agnostic Front, were the founders of the hardcore movement along the entire East Coast. All of these bands are to North American punk rock what John Lee Hooker, Robert Johnson, Willie Dixon, Howling Wolf, and BB King were to the blues. They were the leaders that paved the way and influenced all those who followed. There have been thousands upon thousands of great punk bands throughout the world. Some became popular, while other excellent punk bands have remained obscure. For *American Hardcore* to include

Battalion of Saints

Battalion of Saints as among the best is humbling. For the record, I don't put a lot of stock in using the word "best" to describe **any** bands, punk or otherwise, because there are just way too many fantastic bands across so many different genres to call any one of them the best. My point is only that Battalion of Saints was highly regarded and very well respected.

The sad truth was that I was a 21-year-old drummer with a newly minted, and realistically worthless, two-year Associate in Arts degree who was jobless and broke and still living with his parents. I really didn't have anything to lose anyway. I wasn't very familiar with Battalion of Saints other than what Johnny Salton had mentioned to me at Crank's rehearsal eight months prior. A week after that rehearsal, Johnny had played for me a recording of Battalion of Saints playing "Ace of Spades," and man did it sound good! It was a leap of faith, but if I had a chance to join a good touring band, I was going to. On Monday morning, I got on a plane headed for Kennedy Airport, and as soon as I landed, went straight to Johnny Stiff's apartment in Williamsburg. Johnny handed me a boombox, cassette tapes of *Second Coming* and *Fighting Boys*, Battalion of Saints' two best albums, and I locked myself in his guest bedroom to learn all of the songs. Steely Dan it wasn't, but learning 19 songs in one day that you've never heard before is a daunting task. I had to be familiar with every beginning, every break, every change, and every ending, of every song by 9 p.m. that night. I would be expected to not only know the songs, but to play them well. There would be no allowance for a learning curve. It was either impress the band members or be put back on a plane to Miami, which incidentally, they probably wouldn't have paid for.

I arrived at Johnny's in Brooklyn at around noon, which gave me about eight hours to learn the songs. I was an old pro at cramming, so I knew what needed to be done and wasn't bothered too much by the pressure. I played the cassette tapes from start to finish while patting my drumsticks on the bed and my feet on the floor. Then I played each individual song till I felt I kind of knew it before moving on to the next song. For eight straight hours I worked on learning all the songs, stopping only to use the bathroom or to wolf down the turkey and provolone cheese on white bread sandwiches that Johnny was nice enough to bring me from the Polish deli downstairs. Johnny Stiff never seemed to get the credit or attention that he deserved for his contribution to the music scene. He was literally the hardest working and most influential promoter of punk and hardcore in NYC. Johnny had staked his own name and reputation on me and was selflessly helping me, and I for one, greatly appreciated that. At around 8 p.m., I washed my face, grabbed an extra pair of drum sticks, and Johnny and I headed out to the rehearsal studio in midtown Manhattan to meet with the band.

Chris and George, the leaders of Battalion of Saints, barely even looked at me when Johnny introduced us. I wasn't completely certain that I belonged in the studio with them either, so I wasn't offended. I was very concerned that I would not be able to remember the 19 songs that I had just jammed into my brain. It's one thing to play to a recording, no less on a bed and a wooden floor, and another to play live and without the benefit of a soundtrack in the background. The bass player, James Cooper, said hello to me, and maybe it was because he noticed that my sphincter muscle was clenched so tight that my face was beginning to distort, told me to relax, that I would do just fine. I managed a forced smile and took my place behind the drum kit. I told myself, "Fuck it. Fuck these rock stars. I'm gonna blow them fucking away."

I was accustomed to rehearsing in a $5 an hour 10' X 10' room with rinky-dink equipment. We were in a studio that was nicer than some of the clubs I had played at. It was a bona-fide sound stage that must have been 50' long and 30' wide and equipped with top of the line amplifiers and a state-of-the-art P.A. system. The drums were perched on a drum riser that placed me about 2' above the band. I had been told that Jimi Hendrix had rehearsed in that same room. For a lingering moment, I set aside my doubts and focused on the fact that I was in the best rehearsal hall that I had ever played in, with the best and coolest musicians I ever played with. What more could I fucking want?

There wasn't any attempt made to chitchat socially in order to break the ice, and we immediately got down to business. Chris walked over to me and called out the first song, "My Minds Diseased," counted to four, and started the guitar intro to the song. I came in right on time with the sharp, staccato drum roll that leads to the main section of the song, and as the song continued, it occurred to me that I was playing completely in synch with the bass player, and, that I knew the song. It only takes one song to figure out if all the players in a band are on the same page, and after playing "My Mind's Diseased," it was apparent that I fit in. For three hours we practiced all of the songs, and somewhere along the way, it transitioned from an audition, to more of a "Let's teach the new drummer our songs" session. Often, Chris or George would call out the next song and I would have to ask, "Which one is that," or, "How does that one start?" There was no way to have known ahead of time if I would be able to remember the songs I had learned earlier that same day, but after running through all of the songs with the band, it turned out that I did know them. Maybe not by name, but I knew every beginning, every break, every change, and every ending. Now I needed to work on playing the songs smoothly and powerfully, and to learn the songs by name, as I would not be able to ask George, "Hey, which one is that?" at live concerts. Because of the adrenalin that flows and the

Battalion of Saints

absolute bedlam in the pit and on stage, playing live is a whole different animal than playing in a studio. The good news was that we had booked the studio for another rehearsal the following night. The bad news was that the tour began on Wednesday, which was the night that followed. That still would not give me ample time to properly learn all of the songs.

Regardless of how ready I was or wasn't, on Wednesday afternoon we loaded our equipment into the 1973 Dodge Sportsman van that the band had recently purchased and took off for Stamford. Our first gig was at a club named Anthrax, and it was expected to be a big event. For the most part I knew the songs, but definitely lacked the confidence that is essential to play the songs well and to have fun in the process. Forget about making the songs "my own" or being entertaining while playing them. That was still far off. For now, I just needed to make it to the end of each song without screwing up too badly. Chris and George never formally said that I was the official drummer and were still not interacting with me. I didn't think too much of it because I was stressed about learning all the songs and would just let our relationship progress naturally. Many years later, I found out that the reason they weren't interacting with me was because there was still some debate as to whether or not they were even going to keep me as the drummer. Chris Smith's cousin, who was a drummer, had played the first Battalion of Saints show of the Northeast tour, which had actually begun at The Cuando Center in NYC on August 4th, two days before I had even arrived. The Cuando show featured an impressive line-up of bands, including Agnostic Front, and had been a major NYC hardcore matinee event. By all accounts, due to Chris's cousin not being up to the task, Battalion of Saints was absolutely horrible. Johnny Stiff, who had booked the show, offered to introduce the band to a drummer that might help them sound better…me. And although Chris was against it,

Battalion of Saints

George insisted, and had Johnny contact me the very next day and fly me out the day after. Even after my audition, Chris was still trying to convince George and James that his cousin would do better the next time. Hence, the cold-shoulder treatment.

There were two bands playing before us at Anthrax, so the roadies set up our equipment towards the back of the small stage. The opening acts had their equipment in front of ours, and off to the side. There was an overwhelming amount of activity, and the stage was crowded with equipment. As crazy as it may sound, my clumsiness and aggressiveness solidified my place with Battalion of Saints. Not just as a hired drummer, but as full-fledged member of the band. In my haste to get to my drum set in order to make the final adjustments, I knocked over the opening band's guitar amplifier head. I was completely sober and clear-headed, but I am however, clumsy. It wasn't even a big deal, but one of their band members ran up and got in my face about knocking over his rig. He was going ballistic on me, so finally, I just gave him a hard shove and he fell backwards and landed on his drummer's drum kit, knocking over the drums and cymbals. When he got back up to his feet, I squared up to fight, but he only just screamed at me that I was crazy, and then went about picking up the equipment with the help of the other members of his band. I walked away and it ended there, but you know how these things go. It was my first show with Battalion of Saints and I had shoved the opening band's guitar player through the drum set. The club was getting really crowded, and lots of people were giving me funny looks. By the time I ran into George again, I'm not even sure what he had heard, but he was really jazzed up, and slapped me on the shoulder enthusiastically. He had obviously heard about what had happened, and it turned out that I fit right in with those crazy fuckers. When it came time to play, I made a few mistakes, but for the most part, we sounded good. After the show, George and

Battalion of Saints

Chris included me in the interviews from the local fanzines and made it official. I was the new drummer of Battalion of Saints. And so started the wildest and most fun ride of my life!

Chris Smith and George Flores Anthony were my buddies and pals. George was the singer and Chris was the guitar player, and together, they wrote all of the music and lyrics for Battalion of Saints. Although they both thought that they were far different from each other, they had more in common than not. Both George and Chris had intense stage presence, which meant they were entertaining as fuck. Chris was a tall, thin, blond, blue-eyed, German/Irish looking, fully tattooed, incredibly talented, punk guitar god, and George was a dark haired, thick, scary, dramatic looking singer, who wore fishnet stockings underneath his ripped black jeans, and danced like an erratic, convulsing Elvis while he sang. You might say that George was in touch with his feminine side. Between George Anthony's intense, high-shrieked vocals and hip shaking, and Chris Smith's Hendrix inspired, eyebrow raising guitar work, they were, as I've already elegantly described, entertaining as fuck. When I first joined them, my sole focus was just on not ruining the songs. Less than a year later, the manic, but effective way that I drummed placed me as an equal focal point for the audience to watch. I looked as if I was completely out of control, but every single note that needed to be played, was played. To make the drumming interesting and unpredictable, I rarely played the accents on the drums and cymbals that they were expected to be played on. Other than hitting the obligatory two and four beats on the snare drum with my left hand and thumping the bass drum in time with the bass line, I didn't even know ahead of time myself what else I was going to play. It was as if the songs were moving my feet, arms, and wrists to play what they were supposed to play. If you were watching me, there was no way you could figure out exactly what I was doing… it was too fast. But your ears

Battalion of Saints

confirmed that it sounded not only correct, but powerful as well. When the band was really hitting on all cylinders, I would try to push the pace until we were on the verge of spiraling out of control. Not just the speed, but the way we played the songs as well. It would have been easy to play the songs as recorded on the albums or practiced in the studio, but the reward of pushing the songs to the brink by improvising, would be that audiences would pick up on what we were doing and go absolutely crazy. At that point, I'm not sure if we were inspiring the audience or if they were inspiring us. If you listen to the live tracks on *Battalion of Saints Live at CBGB 1984* (which was actually recorded in late spring of 1985), you'll understand what I mean. Every single note of every song is played with feeling and passion. The crowd in the sardine box packed CBGB was going absolutely wild. They were bumping into Chris and Scarlet as they played their guitars and yelling all the lyrics into the microphones. It was total pandemonium. Listen to "Ace of Spades" from that CD. It will feel as if you're in a barrel falling from the lip at the top of Niagara Falls. Although we come close to going out of control and crashing, we manage to keep the song together all the way to the end. But man is it exciting! The legendary Ian Fraser Kilmister from Motörhead, Lemmy of course, who wrote "Ace of Spades," loved the way we played it. Lemmy, Chris, and George once spent a long long weekend at The Jane Hotel shooting up crank (English speed) and drinking whiskey when Motörhead was in town to play at The Rock Hotel. Lemmy, and his girl friend Gil Weston, both commented that Battalion of Saints were one of the few bands that played Ace of Spades really well. Lemmy was the baddest mutha in the history of rock and roll, and "Ace of Spades" has always been my all-time favorite song. "The only card I need...is the ace of spades, the ace of spades!"

Until the middle of the 1985 summer tour, the bass player of Battalion of Saints was James Cooper. Afterwards, Captain

Scarlet (David Lloyd) replaced him. Both James, and then later Scarlet, in completely different ways, balanced out the band. James was a young surfer dude who just acted like himself on stage and let his silky smooth bass playing and boyish surfer good looks do the talking. He was very flowing and highly dependable, which was difficult at the fast speeds that our songs were played. His prowess made it easy for me to take chances on the drum parts because I knew James' bass would always be there to catch me. Scarlet on the other hand, was a step below James playing wise, but was visually striking and more active as he played. He was a 6'4", 235 lb. Londoner with his head shaved on the sides and a thick, elephant turd looking dreadlock in the middle of his head. He wore cool, obscure English band T-shirts with the sleeves cut off and black leather pants tucked into his knee-high, black paratrooper boots. He was an intimidating and entertaining force. He was not blessed with the same ease of playing possessed by James, but damn if he didn't play every note as it should be played. Captain Scarlet, who was our tour manager at the time, convinced George and Chris to kick James out of the band so that he could replace him. It happened in the parking lot of a motel that we were staying at outside of Washington, D.C., and it wasn't pretty. James, who probably didn't get to 150 lbs. soaking wet, was never easily intimidated by anyone. But challenging Scarlet didn't turn out very well for him. I liked James very much, and although I had reluctantly told George and Chris to choose whomever they wanted to play bass, I didn't feel James should get his ass kicked in addition to being kicked out of the band, so I grabbed Scarlet in a bear hug and shepherded him to the van before James could get really hurt. As if nothing had happened, a moment later we were on the way to the next city and the next show, with a frazzled James left behind in our wake. As charismatic and entertaining as Scarlet was, I would never have allowed Chris and George to boot out James if Scarlet was not up to snuff musically. But with

Battalion of Saints

Scarlet on stage, Battalion of Saints was exciting to listen to and even more exciting to watch. James was immediately picked up to tour and record with the outstanding band, The Meatmen, and I saw him happily playing at The Ritz in NYC only a few months later. That's how talented James was.

After the show in Stamford, we had one week off before we were scheduled to play four back-to-back shows in Hartford, western Massachusetts, Boston, and then Providence. We returned back to New York that night feeling pretty good about the state of the band, and George dropped me off at Sonnie and Rose's apartment, which was now on Washington Street in Hoboken, New Jersey, to crash on their couch. I would become pretty good at sleeping on couches, or floors, or whatever. I would become pretty comfortable brushing my teeth every three or four days and going a week or longer without taking a shower or washing my clothes. The human body is truly amazing and can adapt to almost anything. My teeth stayed healthy and I never had bad breath, and although I didn't smell good, I didn't smell too bad either. At least that's what I thought! The contact lenses that were supposed to be taken out of my eyes and cleaned daily went weeks at a time without disinfection. From time to time my eyes would get a pink eye infection, but my optometrist in Miami, who had been my eye doctor since I was a child, would be kind enough to overnight me the ophthalmologic drops that would take care of the problem. I had traveled to NYC with a dozen pairs of drum sticks, the blue jeans, underwear, and belt that were on my body, two T-shirts with the sleeves cut off, one to wear and one to play with, and the socks and boots that covered my feet. That's it. I played each night with bare feet, so my socks always stayed dry, but every time I drummed, my pants and underwear would be soaked with sweat. After Stamford, I jettisoned my underwear. There would be nothing between me and my jeans for the next 14 months. I was turning into a road dog! A dog doesn't need much to be happy. As a matter of fact, the less we had and the simpler we kept it, the better off we were. All those creature comforts you take for granted? Gone. It was time to get on the road, and on a few planes, and tour the world… awooooo!

Road Dogs

When you're on the road, you have nothing in common with the people in the towns that you are in. We didn't look like anybody else, and aside from the obvious hygiene differences, which sound much worse than they really are, we didn't ever watch TV or go to the movies, and we never had the opportunity to build any kind of long standing relationships, because every day or two, it was off to another city. These are in addition to a long list of other notable differences that segregated us from the conventional population. Everywhere in town that we went, pretty much everyone would be watching us, and of course wondering what kind of trouble we were about to cause. Truth is, we were never looking to cause any trouble, unless of course trouble came looking for us, which it definitely did from time to time. I often felt bad for everybody else. Nobody was as free as we were. We were truly enjoying our lives. Is life about watching a TV program? Is life about pretending you enjoy going to work everyday? Fuck that. We thought we were good enough to make some real money at one point or another in the future, but that wasn't on our minds yet at all. We just wanted to travel from city to city, partying with every person that enjoyed our music, and play rock and roll. What more could a 21-year-old drummer want than that?

So back into the van we went.... Hartford on Thursday and western Massachusetts on Friday night. Both of those shows had a strange vibe, because although the crowd was really into it and moshed intensely, I got the impression that these kids were from nice, suburban homes. It seemed markedly different than the

Road Dogs

scene in NYC, which was very "street" and felt very dangerous. As a matter of fact, in western Massachusetts we played in an actual suburb. There were lush trees and nice houses painted white with proverbial white picket fences in front. It was strange, but also comforting and relaxing. We were put up overnight in a nice, two-story home. I slept on the couch downstairs with my pants on. They hadn't come off my body since leaving Hoboken. The next morning, my crotch was on fire! I wish I could tell you that it was a gift from a hot, adoring fan, but it wasn't. I didn't even come close to getting laid the entire time that I was on those East Coast tours. It was a time span from the beginning of August to the beginning of January. How is that possible you ask? Surely the road abounds with carnal opportunities for a cool punk rocker? It does, but I wasn't a cool punk rocker.... yet. At every stage of my musical development I had pushed the boundaries to act the part of who I really was. But truthfully, this was the majors, and I was still a minor leaguer. It was as if a tornado had swooped me up and dropped me into this new, fast-track life. The only way to survive was to take it one step at a time. Right now, it was about continuing to improve the way I drummed to the songs and figuring out how to deal with being on the road all the time. Believe it or not, getting laid, while always a thought, was not a priority. And literally, right now, it was actually all about finding some jock itch cream to cool down my burning crotch!

George came down the stairs with a big grin on his face because he had slept in the bed of the attractive, 30-something-year-old owner of the house. His gloating face implied, "This is how you do it son. One day, you'll get to sleep on a bed, with a woman." My facial reply was of course, "Congratulations fucker!" When I told him of the discomfort I was in, he laughed and said, "That's what you get for leaving your pants on every night dummy!"

Road Dogs

On the way to Boston we stopped at an old-fashioned pharmacy that looked like it was from the 1950's, and I finally bought some Tinactin cream. Ahhhhh... relief.

The Paradise Rock Club in Boston was the coolest club I had ever seen in my life. It was a classic rock and roll concert hall with top-of-the-line sound and lighting systems. Inside, it was uniquely shaped like a baseball diamond, and the stage represented home plate. I guess they love their baseball in Boston! I was on cloud nine in anticipation of playing on the same stage that so many of my favorite rock and roll bands had played on. Paradise is very well known for hosting a who's who of the greatest bands before they became too big to play there anymore. It was the first place U2 played at in the United States. It was exciting to see Fenway Park on the ride over, and it was exciting to be headlining in Boston at this remarkable venue.

Towards the end of that long Saturday afternoon matinee, the place was busting at the seams, and when Corrosion of Conformity started to play, I instantly had the same, "Why are they opening for us?" epiphany as when Agnostic Front opened up for Menstrual Cycle. The band played complex riffs without sacrificing any intensity. Each member of the band was a musician's musician and the drummer was especially magnificent. My immediate impressions proved to be correct. Corrosion of Conformity has stayed together for many years and is very well respected worldwide. We went on right after and put on an exciting show of our own. Our songs were a little catchier, a little more sing-along than Corrosion's, so we weren't better or worse than they were, just different. I am confident that everyone who paid admission that day felt like they got their money's worth. That night, we partied in Boston for a while and then took the train to a party in South Boston. Never going back

Road Dogs

to South Boston again! Just take my word; those Southies are fucking crazy. You've been warned.

The next morning, we left for Providence to play a Sunday matinee, and later that night, I was dropped off in Hoboken. I was glad that Rose and Sonnie were letting me sleep on their couch because our next gig wasn't until two weeks later, when Battalion of Saints would be headlining the Sunday Hardcore Matinee at CBGB. Because of the way they had bombed at The Cuando Center earlier that summer, it was a crucial show.

I had absolutely nothing to do for those two weeks. James took a train to D.C., where his father lived, and Chris and George disappeared into the city to get into whatever trouble they could get into or do whatever drugs they could get their hands on. Left by myself, I hung out at the Park Inn on E. 9th street and Avenue A with the local punks and skinheads. Park Inn was an old-school bar where we would see Joe Jackson sitting by himself and drinking almost every night. Crazy, violent fights would spontaneously break out and then thankfully, would be quickly quashed by the colorful bouncer, Ike the Dyke. Afterwards, some of us would walk the two blocks to the Holiday lounge, the greatest dive bar in NYC, to drink $1.50 Jack and Cokes. Late night, we'd stumble into the Pyramid Club or A7 to see great thrash bands playing three feet in front of our faces. More often than not, we would all end up by the benches at Tomkins Square Park across the street on Avenue A, drinking quarts of cheap malt liquor till the sun came up. Somebody was always nice enough to let me crash at their apartment, so I wouldn't have to trek all the way back to Hoboken. It was a unique and exciting time to be in Manhattan's East Village. History was being made, and we will never see anything like what existed on Avenue A in the early 1980's ever again. Soulless corporations like

Road Dogs

Starbucks and The Gap, that now own every corner and every street down there, will make sure of that.

September 2nd finally arrived and it was time for Battalion of Saints to redeem themselves in NYC. With the memory of the horrendous performance one month earlier fresh on everyone's mind, it was a case of "earn our respect or we'll stomp you this time!" We took the stage, and the danger was very real and standing right in front of us in the form of 75 amped up skinheads. The audiences at the CBGB Sunday Hardcore Matinees were so intimidating and so tightly wound that in an instant, their fervent support could turn into violent retaliation over the slightest provocation. The moment we started playing, everyone could tell that this was a different band. This was the real Battalion of Saints! We killed it. We left a very happy crowd at CBGB. I already couldn't wait to play there again.

Next on our schedule was a European tour. We had shows booked throughout England and Italy, and once we were overseas, more cities would easily be added on. Our first show was scheduled for October 22nd in London on the same bill as Hanoi Rocks, Johnny Thunders, and The Addicts. As excited as I was to play on such a loaded bill, what was I supposed to do for five weeks? I don't mind some mindless partying every now and again, but I had already been doing that the past two weeks, and that was enough.

If you immerse yourself in New York City, it's bound to rub off on you, and I felt like I was beginning to understand the ways of New York a little better. I used the downtime to expand my limited wardrobe. At a thrift store in the Village, I found a faded, sleeveless jean jacket that was totally rock and roll, two pairs of pants, one black and one that was an interesting light-lime-green color, and a couple of shirts, one which was long-sleeved,

Road Dogs

because the temperature was starting to cool down a bit. It wasn't enough to bog me down on the road but went a long way towards sprucing up my look and to raising my own self-esteem. The long-sleeved shirt, worn un-tucked over a T-shirt, made it slightly easier to fit in around "normal" people. Sonnie continued to help me out. She showed me how to use a crimping iron and how to tease my full head of black hair with a comb to make it look wilder, and she bought me my first can of Aqua Net Super Hold hairspray. It was all much-needed progress. At times, the five idle weeks seemed to drag, but the wait finally came to an end. Next stop: Europe.

Unfortunately, unless you are a super-mega band, which we were not, nothing ever goes as smoothly as planned, and delays and disappointment are always part of the landscape. We got on that British Airways flight at Kennedy airport beyond stoked to be headed towards London to play an extended European tour. Just imagine how good we were all feeling; we were on the way to play a massive show in London…**London fucking England**, and then continuing on to play from city to city in Europe for the next 30 days or more!

We landed in Heathrow Airport and walked through customs feeling, and looking, like the top American band that we were. And that's when the situation quickly headed south. The entire band was intercepted and then escorted by extra-large customs officers into a room just past the customs area, where we were met by our tour manager from London, Scarlet, and an official looking immigrations officer. I assumed it was just the normal bullshit of a strange looking rock band getting hassled a little bit, but it turned out to be much worse than that. The immigrations officer had in his hand a copy of *Melody Maker* (the *Rolling Stone* of England), and much of the Battalion of Saints tour itinerary was splashed in large letters on the back pages. Since we didn't

Road Dogs

have work visas, we were screwed. The inquiry, or better said, inquisition, lasted 15 minutes, and the outcome was that we would be put on the next available flight back to Kennedy. They put an X through the entrance stamp on my passport, and that was that. We were kicked out of England. Scarlet had brought along a fifth of Jack Daniels with him and we drained it in the holding room. When the oversized customs officers came back to escort us to the awaiting plane that would return us to NYC, we were totally wasted, and George and I spat in the faces of the officers, calling them "Fucking Limeys." Like I said, I fit right in with these crazy fuckers! I'm not proud of my behavior, but my actions were totally spontaneous. I hate mindless bureaucracy. We wouldn't have taken anybody's job, so not letting us in the country was just total bullshit. I passed out while the plane was still taxiing on the runway before takeoff.

The bad news was that the band was now out of money and that we obviously didn't have any more shows booked. This meant everybody had to go home. The three other guys flew home to San Diego, and I flew back to Miami. The good news?

Well…there just wasn't any good news.

The End of the Road?

Do I really have to tell you how much it sucked to be back in Florida? I didn't think so! On October 11th, at 6 a.m. I had flown to London in anticipation of the greatest 30 days of my life. On October 12th, only 18 hours later, I was back at Miami International Airport, waiting for a ride back to my parents' house. Was this really happening?

Maybe it was because I was not in a great state of mind, but the next day, Friday, I woke up with my mind racing. I needed to make some money, and I wanted to play a show with Crank again. I called Elaine and told her that I would be in town for a while. She was surprised to hear from me, but was confident that Richard Shelter, the promoter at Flynn's, would be happy to book us. My next phone call was to the guy that had hooked me up to unload the marijuana boat when I was with The Spinouts. He told me that there was plenty of work available, and that he would contact me as soon as I was needed. In a very unhealthy way, I felt as if I had to make up for some lost time.

Finally, I called George Anthony in California. In those days, in order to make a long-distance phone call from a public phone, you had to tell the operator your long-distance code number and she would then provide you with a phone line to make your call on. That made it very easy to steal other people's long-distance codes. All you had to do was pretend you were making a phone call on the next phone over and write down the other guy's code when he said it out loud to the operator. We had an endless supply of stolen codes to make free long-distance phone calls

The End of the Road?

with, and so I was able to speak with George in California anytime I wanted to. When I told him what I was doing to earn some money, he cautioned me to be careful and that we were far from done touring. The very next day, on Saturday morning, I got a call to work the following evening on a crew. I accepted the job. The house where the pot laden boat was scheduled to arrive at was on North Shore Drive in Normandy Shores, five minutes away from my parents' house in North Bay Village. When I spoke to George that Saturday afternoon, he again told me not to do it. He told me another tour was already in the works. I laughed, as if either I didn't believe him, or that the risk didn't bother me. Actually, both were true; I didn't think it was possible to magically arrange another tour after the total evaporation of the European tour, and, I really wasn't too concerned about getting caught unloading a pot boat, because the odds were with me. Only a very small percentage of boats carrying contraband got pinched getting into South Florida.

The next afternoon, on Sunday at around 4 p.m., I showed up at the address that I was told to go to. It was an up-scale home directly on Biscayne Bay right across from the posh homes of Biscayne Point. As the night progressed, I reminisced about how cool it was to have unloaded the previous pot boat and the rush I got from doing it. I wanted to feel that again, and I wanted the $2,000 paycheck the job now paid. At the same time, I was absolutely torn by the thought of what I was risking. I had been badly affected by the European tour being snatched away from me. But, all in all, how fucking awesome of a summer had it been? The next morning at 7 a.m., I was relieved when we were told to go home after **not** having unloaded a boat. That night, when I told George that I was no longer considering any more crew work, he scolded that I had been an idiot to even do it once.

The End of the Road?

The very next day, George called to let me know that we were back in business. The band would be meeting in Washington, D.C. later in the week, and our first show was on Friday. Exactly a short week after being kicked out of England, we were booked to play an extensive tour of DC, Maryland, Pennsylvania, Upstate New York, North Carolina, South Carolina, Atlanta, and Virginia. The tour started on October 18th and would end the second week of December. While we were on that tour, we were notified that an **additional tour** had been inked, making us the opening band for the English band Broken Bones, which would take us across the country from New York City to Los Angeles. That tour was set to commence on New Year's Eve at The Rock Hotel in NYC. We were road dogs again for sure!

All of these changes of events had occurred remarkably quickly. To complicate matters, Elaine, upon my own prompting, had booked a show in Miami Beach for Friday, October 26th, the same day Battalion of Saints was booked in Philadelphia. I could have easily said sorry to Crank and to Richard Shelter, but that's not the way I roll. A commitment is a commitment. I asked George to cancel the Philadelphia show so that I could fly in to Miami for the Crank show. The following night after the Crank show, I would then meet the band in Pittsburgh to play at The Electric Banana.

As planned, a week into the tour, after playing a concert in Syracuse, the band dropped me off at Philadelphia Airport so I could fly to Miami. The gig with Crank was an emotional homecoming for me. Many of the people there that night knew me from back in The Reactions days and were excited that I was now touring nationally with Battalion of Saints. The heartfelt show of support was not lost on me. Crank played exceptionally well and I was glad that I made the effort to be there. The very next night, I was off to Pittsburgh.

The End of the Road?

I arrived at West Palm Beach airport dressed to go directly to The Electric Banana right after landing at Pittsburgh International Airport. I was wearing those funky, light-lime-green colored pants tucked into my combat boots and my hair was teased to give it that tussled, dirty rock and roll look. I was accustomed to getting strange looks wherever I went, and the waiting area of the airport in West Palm Beach was no exception. I scoped out the area and noticed a beautiful, well-dressed, blonde girl who was maybe 20, 21 years of age, who was doing her best to ignore me. Okay, she was ignoring me, but in my mind, that required an effort on her part! She seemed to be travelling by herself, so when we boarded the plane, I sat one seat away from her on the aisle seat, and she sat in the window seat. I wanted to show interest, without appearing 'stalky.' The People's Express flight, which didn't assign seats ahead of time, was relatively full, but fortunately, nobody sat between us.

This girl was absolutely gorgeous, and although she seemed too classy to go for a guy like me, I just had to give it a shot. When I was living in San Diego a few months later, she mailed me a few Polaroids of herself in different poses, which definitely confirmed my recollection of what she looked like. She was a young, blonde, Canadian natural beauty! Anyway, chit led to chat, and when we ordered a round of beers together, I moved one seat over to be closer to her. By the time the flight attendant had brought us our second round of beers, I was feeling a connection, and so I offered her one of the Quaaludes that were in my pocket. She surprisingly popped it without hesitation right into her mouth, and I popped one as well.

While I had been in Miami, I had finagled 20 Swiss Quaaludes to turn the guys on to. They would be so happy! Since I had not checked in any luggage, I had them all in a baggy that was

The End of the Road?

shoved into my front pants pocket. Before we were even done with our second beers, about an hour into the flight now, we started making out like it was our last day on earth. As calmly and as coolly as possible given the heated circumstances, I reached up and grabbed a blanket from the overhead bin, and we managed to do everything possible underneath that blanket that we possibly could have done, until the plane began its descent into Pittsburgh International Airport. She was staying on the plane, which was continuing to Ontario, and I was getting off, so she gave me her phone number and I promised to contact her if we played anywhere near her.

I disembarked from the plane and ambled towards the baggage claim area. I was really feeling the two beers and the Quaalude, but fortunately, Chris located me and scurried me to the van that George had waiting on the ramp. The plane had been an hour late in taking off and the band was now late to go on stage. George drove like a maniac so that in less than a half-hour, we walked straight out of the van and directly onto the stage at the very crowded Electric Banana. Although I was as wasted as Tommy Chong in the scene from the movie Cheech and Chong, when Chong (also high on ludes) is falling over the drum kit during the battle of the bands, as soon as those drumsticks were in my hands and Chris had counted off the first song, I was good to go. After the show, I was handed an Iron City beer and we all walked over to get us some of the best Philly cheesesteaks that I've still ever had.

The rest of the tour went well. Every day or two we would travel to another city and another show. It was all about building goodwill in the towns and bars that we played in. The locals were always happy to see a good West Coast band and treated us really well. Once the tour was over, we holed up for two weeks in the D.C. area, where everybody had a convenient place

The End of the Road?

to stay. This time around I crashed with James and our clean-cut, all-American, but yet mean-ass roadie, Rich, at my cousins Ela and Ralph's apartment in Maryland while they were away. Not only were we warm and comfortable, but we had the use of a car as well. The tour had worked out very well, and we all enjoyed the much-needed break.

Punk Rock Winter

Early afternoon on December 31st, we boarded our trustworthy Dodge van for the drive back to NYC for the opening night of a nine-city tour as the supporting act for the popular English band, Broken Bones. The tour would take us from NYC to LA in 18 days, with shows in NYC, Richmond, Newport, Chicago, Denver, Las Vegas, San Diego, Phoenix, and LA.

But tonight it was New Year's Eve, so before heading into the City, we gathered at Chris's sister's house in Queens for some celebrating. George Anthony, a culinary school trained gourmet chef, treated us to a spectacular sushi and sashimi dinner. We were all feeling upbeat in anticipation of the show that evening and of the upcoming tour. At around 8 o'clock, as we were getting ready to leave Queens, I decided to contribute to the festivities by handing out five Quaaludes each to James, Chris, and George. Tonight was the perfect night to partake in the Swiss Quaaludes that I had brought back from Miami.

As noble as my intentions were, those Quaaludes got us into a remarkable amount of trouble, which could have turned out much, much worse. Of course, George blamed me for giving Chris the five Quaaludes, but I never would have imagined that Chris was going to take them all before we played at 11 p.m. Who takes five Quaaludes all at once and expects to function?

This was a massive New Year's Eve show. The line-up was Murphy's Law, Circle Jerks, Battalion of Saints, and Broken Bones. Any one of those bands, by themselves, could have filled

Punk Rock Winter

the 1,300-person capacity Rock Hotel. Murphy's Law was a very popular NYC band that combined ferocious hardcore music with very catchy songs and highly entertaining sing-along interludes. Circle Jerks were the quintessential Los Angeles punk band, and Broken Bones was a first-rate English band that was cut in the same mold as fellow British bands, Discharge and GBH. It was a stacked show and every skinhead and punk rocker in the tri-state area crawled out of their hiding holes to be there that night.

This was not the night that you wanted the voluminous, rabid crowd to turn against you, but that's exactly what happened. Because of the five Quaaludes that he had taken, by the fourth song, Chris was stumbling around and playing his guitar very sloppy. I was still not overly concerned because Chris could normally handle playing even when very fucked up and would surely straighten up to finish the set. In the meantime, a hole opened up on my snare drum head, and you can't drum with a hole in your snare drum! I quickly went to the side of the stage and grabbed Murphy's Law drummer, Petey's, snare drum. He started to object, but I hissed at him that I knew some asshole had cut my snare drum on purpose, and that I was fucking borrowing his whether he liked it or not. Me and Petey weren't friends yet, but we knew each other from when I was hanging out on Avenue A, and so with a guilty look on his face, he threw his hands up in the air and told me to just take it.

When I got back to my drum set to replace the snare drum, I could see three burly skinheads standing around Chris. These guys were 100% straight edge, meaning they were opposed to alcohol and drugs, and were noticeably pissed at Chris's inebriated behavior. This was really bad, and I was seriously concerned not just for the safety of Chris, but for my own as well. I could feel the level of anger rising rapidly in the crowd.

Punk Rock Winter

Right before the start of the next song, one of the skinheads threw a roundhouse kick at Chris, but as the song started, the three skinheads jumped off the stage. Chris was now barely able to keep from falling over, and so when the song finished, George gave the "we're done" sign, and we all got off the stage quickly. I was very happy to leave that stage unscathed because I had also taken a Quaalude, just one mind you, and so would not have been at my best to handle any violence. Chris's girlfriend escorted him home. George and James, not taking any chances, also left. Probably because of the time I had spent hanging out with the locals back in August and September, it turned out nobody was mad at me, and so I ended up staying at Rock Hotel till 5 a.m., and thoroughly enjoyed my New Year's Eve. Afterwards, Captain Scarlet, who was the road manager of Broken Bones, and I grabbed a cab and shared a hotel room at the dodgy, inexpensive Iroquois Hotel on 44th Street in Midtown. This was when Times Square was a decadent, dangerous area, not the make-believe, tourist district that it is now. The next day, January 1st, was a travel day, so George Anthony and I hit the road to Richmond, Virginia.

The band was road hardened from being constantly on the road for the last five months. My hygiene routine hadn't changed too much, but my body had become accustomed to it, and I felt great. No rashes, no health issues, nothing. I was strong like bull! The travel arrangements for the cross-country tour were that George and I would ride in our Dodge van with all of the equipment, and everybody else would ride in a leased, late model, comfy, eight-passenger Ford van. The tires on the Dodge van, which had already seen their fair share of miles, were worn thin, and we had already skidded once on the way to a show in December, when the roads were a bit icy. It was cold, in the upper 20's, but at least the weather was clear.

Punk Rock Winter

Our first stop was the pre-civil war Landmark Theatre in Richmond, which was an incredible place to play. It was the kind of building where you were more likely to see a Shakespearean play or hear a Mozart concert, rather than a punk show. Very classy. The next three shows found us in Newport, Kentucky, which is just across the river from Cincinnati, Chicago, and then cross-country to Denver. Although the weather was clear in the Northeast, a cold front had dumped large amounts of snow throughout the West and Midwest, which was where we were headed in our worn-out, old van.

When we got to Chicago, the winds were whipping and the snow was piled 4-feet high on the sides of the roads. We played at a gorgeous, ornate, concert hall called Metro, which was on North Clark Street, only a quarter mile away from Wrigley Field, home of The Chicago Cubs. You need to imagine yourself in my shoes. Six months ago, I was playing at a 27 Birds Lounge in Coconut Grove, Florida, and now this? A few years later, Nirvana and Smashing Pumpkins would play at Metro. Backstage we were treated to a lavish buffet and plenty of beer and alcohol, and there were reporters and photographers interviewing the bands and snapping lots of pictures. It was all very cool, but it was also very strange. We were two punk bands...and this scene was so not punk rock. I got the urge to start doing shots of Jack Daniels with beer chasers, so I went with it. **That** was punk rock!

As we played that night, I took in, and was mesmerized by everything that I was seeing...the beautiful stage, the sweeping balconies, and the sold-out concert hall. I had a few more beers while Broken Bones played, and right after they finished, I decided to pop my next-to-last Quaalude and hang out in the lobby while the venue emptied out, serenely observing the departing crowd and enjoying the moment. We were playing

Punk Rock Winter

across the country in Denver in two nights, so I knew we had to leave as soon as the equipment was all put away in the van. I had a great buzz going and was loose as a goose. Thirty minutes later, after the place had emptied out, George asked me if I was ready, and we walked together to the van. George told me that he was tired and asked if I wouldn't mind driving the first shift. As you already know, Quaaludes rarely inspire one to make the right choice, so I said, "Sure," and got behind the wheel of the van to head southwest towards Denver.

Before you freak out that I was driving while I was obviously impaired, please remember this was 1985, and driving under the influence (DUI) laws were dramatically more lenient than they are now. Furthermore, I drove for many hours on an almost daily basis as we travelled from city to city and was an excellent long-range driver. Finally, if I were really that fucked up, which I wasn't, I would have asked George to drive for a few hours till I straightened up. I took the wheel at around 12:30 a.m. and we headed due south from Chicago towards Springville, Illinois. The heater was blowing, but considering that it was maybe nine degrees outside, it wasn't exactly toasty in the old van.

Two and a half hours later on the dark, 18-wheeler dominated road, I noticed that the fuel gauge was near empty. No problem. I would just find a gas station. I passed a number of gas stations, but none of them were open, so I kept on driving until I reached Williamsville, a small town just before Springfield, and pulled into a big truck stop. I couldn't risk running out of gas on the highway, which we were already close to doing. I got out of the van to learn that the gas pumps didn't open till 6 a.m. Again, not a problem, we would just wait till the gas station opened. I pulled the van up by the 18-wheelers that were also waiting to fuel up, and we went to sleep. An hour later, George and I both woke up shivering from the cold. The heater was no longer

Punk Rock Winter

blowing hot air. We had run out of gas! This was a real problem. The gas pumps wouldn't open for another two hours and we didn't have blankets or warmer clothing to wear. Remember, we were minimalistic road dogs....awooooo!

We both knew what we had to do, so with very little conversation we crawled into the back of the van, re-arranged some bags that were full of guitar cords and laid down spooning each other on the small space available next to the guitar amplifiers. I know it sounds awkward, but it turned out not to be weird at all. We were in survival mode and were doing what was necessary to literally just survive. We fell back asleep and didn't even move till I woke up at 6:15. George was beginning to get sick, so I handled pouring the gas while George did his best to stay warm.

George angrily took the wheel after we left the truck stop. Understandably, he was pissed-off that I had allowed the van to run out of gas. I had fucked up, and the blame rested squarely on my shoulders. George was getting even sicker now and was running a fever and feeling really uncomfortable. I took the wheel to drive the rest of the way, and was expecting to arrive in Denver by around 9 p.m. At around 7 p.m., when I noticed the fuel gauge reading less than ¼ tank, I started to get that strong feeling of déjà vu. Some of the distances between gas stations in Colorado were 40 miles or more, so if I didn't find an open gas station soon, I was going to run out of gas **again**! It was in the low 20's in Colorado, and George was feeling even worse. "Please don't run out of gas, please don't run out of gas," I chanted to myself, but to no avail. Right after Strasburg, a town about an hour east of Denver, the car putt-putted to the side of the highway, devoid of any gasoline. I was beside myself with an overwhelming feeling of guilt. George was shivering uncontrollably and even hallucinating a bit, so I told him to sit tight and that I would somehow be back with some gasoline.

From the side of the highway, I saw a lit-up gas station in a far-off valley at the bottom of the mountain hill that we were on. The light from the moon was plenty enough to guide me, so I grabbed the red gas can that we had purchased at the Williamsville truck stop and began to jog down the hill towards the gas station. I was in pretty good shape from jogging and exercising almost every day, and we weren't at very high altitude yet, so I could breathe okay. I made good time to the gas station, filled up the gas can, and jogged back up to the car. The guilt kept me running when I was ready to stop and walk, and fortunately, I wasn't attacked by any coyotes in the wild brush. If George had been without heat for too much longer, we would have had a serious medical situation on our hands. I dropped George off with the promoter in Denver, who took him to his own house to try and recover a little bit. The rest of the guys, Chris, Scarlet, Nobby Bones, Tony Bones, Paul Oddy, and Darren "Bazzer" Burgess couldn't believe that I had run out of gas twice in a row and got a good laugh upon hearing it. George showed up the next night for the show feeling only slightly better than the night before. He didn't think it was funny at all.

The show in Denver was a little strained because the Denver Police were there in force and hassled the promoter about everything. Broken Bones and Battalion of Saints played their sets, but the threat of police action cast a gloomy shadow over the performances. After the show, Scarlet and I got an offer to go home with two young girls who looked to be between 18-21 years of age. We both just wanted to get the hell out of there, so we accepted the invitation. Scarlet was an interesting guy. Aside from being 6'4" and having a one-foot long, one-inch thick dreadlock on top of his otherwise shaved head, he also sported

Punk Rock Winter

two nose rings, an eyebrow piercing, a tongue piercing, multiple ear piercings of course, and two piercings directly on his penis. He spoke with a barely discernible English Cockney accent that sounded as if he were speaking with a mouthful of marbles. Although he was very intelligent…he had been the tour manager of some very good English bands, and even ended up working for Siouxsie and The Banshees, he was also very mischievous, and there was no limit to how far he was willing to go. In New Orleans, after Battalion of Saints had performed at Tulane University, we were all partying and drinking Jägermeister at a bar in the French Quarter, and Scarlet and I went outside to get some fresh air.

I daringly said to Scarlet, "Scarlet, let's jump through that store window." Obviously, I was kidding, as it was just a silly, drunk comment.

Scarlet said, "Alright, count to three."

To play along I counted, "One, two, three!"

Scarlet sprinted across the street and flung himself against the window of the storefront! The glass spilled onto the sidewalk, along with Scarlet. The store alarm started ringing loudly and Scarlet was cut and bleeding throughout the entire front of his body. As if by some sixth sense after hearing the alarm, Chris Smith, who was still inside the bar, came out to see what was up, and saw me helping a bloody Scarlet up off of the glass covered sidewalk. He shouted that we had to get Scarlet out of there before the police showed up, and so we took him back to the bar and just continued our night as if nothing had happened. The night ended with Chris, George, and Scarlet being asked to leave from the next bar we went to, right after I had been served the first, and best, blackened redfish that I'd ever had. I got up to leave shaking my head disappointingly, but the owner of the bar said, "No, not you. You can stay and finish your meal. Just the other guys!" And so I got to enjoy my delicious blackened redfish in the French Quarter of New Orleans.

I'm saying that it was possible that Scarlet already knew that these girls were underage. To him of course, that made it even more interesting. I had absolutely no clue that these girls might be younger than they appeared to be until I saw the teenybopper posters on the wall in one of the bedrooms. Shit! I got that sinking feeling that these girls were closer to 18, at best, than to 21. As far as I was concerned, it was game off. I still needed a place to sleep, so that's all I did, sleep. But not Scarlet. Although I don't think too much happened in the way of romance, the next day, one of the underage girls decided to go with him to our next show in Las Vegas, **750 miles away**. She drove in the Ford van with him, and even used her daddy's credit card to buy meals for everyone and gasoline for the van. If this girl had accused us of kidnapping, we would have been royally screwed. The father drove all the way to Las Vegas the next night and picked her up without incident, while everyone stayed out of sight. It doesn't take much of an imagination to picture a drastically different outcome.

Dirty Mama's in Las Vegas was a really nice, modern club and the crowd turned out to be much more animated than I had anticipated. The tour was going very well and both bands were in a good mood. George had almost fully recovered and had gotten over being mad at me for running out of gas, twice. I was looking forward to spending some time in Las Vegas before we shipped out to San Diego the next day, but George told me we were leaving as soon as the equipment was put away. Not only did I want to stay in Las Vegas to have some fun, but an extreme cold front had reached even Las Vegas, and the State Police was

Punk Rock Winter

closing the icy highway from midnight to 6 a.m. to any vehicles that didn't have tire chains. Our tires didn't even have tread! Every icy highway and mountain that we had driven on, with hundreds of pounds of equipment inside of the van, had been terrifying. George wasn't asking me, he was telling me we were getting on that road while we still could. What could be so important in San Diego that George would risk our lives for?

Finally it occurred to me why George was so anxious to leave; there were good drugs in San Diego, and George wasn't waiting an extra 12 hours to get to them. So, being the good friend that I was, and also because I didn't have a choice anyway, I left with George on our bald tires mere minutes before the authorities shut the icy roads down. As a token concession for risking my life, George, who knew I liked to gamble, stopped at Whiskey Pete's right before we crossed the border into California from Nevada, and we enjoyed a celebratory steak dinner and 45 minutes of blackjack. Afterwards, it was straight on I-15 towards Los Angeles where I experienced first-hand the shockingly powerful Santa Ana winds that blew the van over one full lane or more with each gust. As the sun began to rise, we finally reached my brother's house in the North County of San Diego. It was quite the coincidence, and incredibly convenient, that my brother happened to live in the same city that Battalion of Saints was headquartered in. That meant I had a place to stay. Well, kind of.

Shaka Brah...Dude

There were three shows left on the Broken Bones tour; San Diego, Phoenix, and then finally, Los Angeles at the Olympic Auditorium. Steve Jones, the bass player of the most famous and notorious punk band ever, the Sex Pistols, was joining up with the celebrated NYC punk band Kraut and joining Broken Bones and us for the Los Angeles show. We anticipated the Los Angeles show was going to be a very special event. It turned out even bigger than we expected, as more than 5,000 punk rockers filled the auditorium. 5,000 punks in one venue was unfathomable. Even the flyer from that show was a small part of history. The flyer, with Battalion of Saints and Broken Bones clearly visible, shows up in the background of the punk record store scene in the movie *Pretty in Pink*. You have to zoom in to see it, but it's there. 30 Years later, one of the main characters in the blockbuster TV series, *13 Reasons Why*, dons a Battalion of Saints T-shirt during the punk rock scene. Battalion of Saints being represented in both of these epic productions speaks volumes of the longevity and significance of the band.

Six days prior to the LA show, on January 12th, was the San Diego homecoming of Battalion of Saints. It was the return of the hometown heroes after six months on the Northeast Coast. It was also the introduction of their new drummer, me of course, to San Diego. It felt as if I was meeting the in-laws for the first time, and I wanted to make a good first impression. Near the beginning of that energetic and emotional homecoming show at Fairmont Hall in San Diego, Chris introduced Joey Wrecked, from Mee-ami, to the audience. The crowd of almost 1,000 kids,

Shaka Brah...Dude

which was as aggressive and violent as I'd seen anywhere in the country, gave me a warm reception and made me feel welcome. Awwww! When the Bones tour was over, I spent almost three months in San Diego enjoying the hospitality of those locals.

The very next morning after the San Diego show, we drove through the Arizona desert and played two sets, a matinee and a night show, at The Mason Jar in Phoenix. The band had scored some crystal meth the day before and were partying backstage. When the two shows were over, since I had only been drinking for six hours and not doing the crystal meth, I insisted on personally driving the whole way back. Like I said, the bar was set really low. It had been a really long seven-day stretch, and I was exhausted. The tumble weed that was constantly blown across the highway looked like animals crossing the road, which freaked me out for a good portion of the long, 350-mile drive. At around 4 a.m., Chris, whose eyes were wide open from the crystal meth, saw me struggling and offered to drive. "No thanks buddy. I got this!" As tired as I was, I felt I was in better shape to drive than any of my bandmates. The sun finally came up, which made driving easier, and we made it back to San Diego.

We had a few days to kill before the LA show, and that's when I tried crystal meth for the first time. It's some powerful shit! I was at a party in San Diego, and apart from Chris and George, I didn't know anybody else there. They both left the party early on, and I found myself sitting on the couch by myself. The people at the party were nice, and the music playing on the stereo, which was a band that I had never heard, was good, but I was just kind of pathetically sitting there. A guy that I was introduced to earlier, Cliff, asked me if I wanted to do a line of crystal. Having never tried it before, I was hesitant, but finally replied curtly, "Sure." We went into the bathroom and he put out a tiny, quarter-inch line to snort. He explained to me that crystal meth was much stronger than cocaine, and one small line was all that I needed for the entire night. The motherfucker was right! It was as if suddenly my eyes were bright and my tail bushy. Gooood moooorning Vietnam!!! Within a minute or two, I was having a great time with my new good friends at the party. And the music? All of a sudden the music on the stereo, which happened to have been Metallica, was awesome! I had heard **of** Metallica but had never actually heard them. Crystal meth and Metallica go together incredibly well and are a match made in heaven, or better said, hell! For the sake of full disclosure, crystal meth is a nasty, habit forming, hellish drug that destroys your teeth and has destroyed plenty of lives, so I am not an advocate of crystal meth. But after snorting a tiny bump, I had a really good time that night and even met a nice Jewish blonde girl, Kaye, who ended up becoming my sort of steady girlfriend. I thought it would be a nice gesture to turn the guys on to a line of this interesting powder, so the day before the LA show I asked Cliff to get me a quarter gram baggie. It was enough for the four of us, but not enough to get into any real trouble with.

I was looking forward to playing in Los Angeles in the same way as I had been excited to play in NYC for the first time. The audiences in California were much bigger than New York. I was even more jacked up about Los Angeles. As soon as I walked into The Olympic Auditorium, my jaw dropped wide open. This place dwarfed any place that we had ever played at, by far. Ours was not a Bruce Springsteen concert, and playing at a venue that held 9,000 seemed a bit overkill. Then I saw the venue's security force, which looked like a small army, gathered to receive their assignments. How many people were they expecting that night?

Before the sound check we had a photo shoot to contend with, so we were all dressed with hair and make-up done. Yes, everyone

Shaka Brah...Dude

in the band wore some kind of make-up. To quote Mark Knopfler of Dire Straits, "See the little faggot with the earring and the makeup...that little faggot, he's a millionaire."

In other words, we were okay with it, and if that bothered you, then you could fuck off. After the sound check we all went back to the dressing room. I had planned to share the crystal with the entire band, but Chris and George were acting kind of dickish, so James and I decided to do all of it ourselves. Big fucking mistake! Cliff had warned me to only do a little, and as soon as I had done the two lines, I knew it was too much. I immediately got extremely jittery and knew I would have trouble drumming in this condition. The effects of crystal meth, unlike cocaine which wears off quickly, can last eight hours or more, so I needed to slow myself down. I stepped outside of the building onto downtown Los Angeles and bought two hot dogs from a hot dog stand just around the corner, and then went back inside to start drinking beer. Did you have a better idea?

Not only was the meth still prominently in my bloodstream as we took the stage, but when I saw the size of the massive crowd and how insane the mosh pit was, it was also joined by a tidal wave of adrenaline. I could see an ocean of punk rockers, and at any one time, there were ten kids diving off the stage onto the crowd. There were even kids diving off of the PA speakers, some of which were 12-feet high. I played the entire set feeling uncoordinated and weak. The tempo of the songs, already fast, was pushed involuntarily faster, as the muscle memory that I rely on to play was short-circuited. It's nights like these that test the will and the desire of a person to get the job done no matter what challenges or difficulties they are presented with. I didn't play well, but I made it through the set, and unless you were hyper-tuned into how it was supposed to have sounded, you

Shaka Brah...Dude

would have hardly noticed the difference. Is it possible to be both embarrassed and proud of the same performance?

Backstage I had met a very attractive blonde girl who was the singer of a band that performed at The Olympic the week before. She was effortlessly cool and beautiful, and as the lead singer, also very poised and personable as well. She stuck around as Battalion of Saints played, and afterwards, while Kraut was playing, I asked her to accompany me to go and buy a pint of Jack Daniels. The scene outside of The Olympic was totally cray-cray! There were cops battling groups of kids that were throwing bottles at them. It was total fucking chaos. I just wanted some Jack Daniels and didn't want to get involved with the hostilities, so we ever so nonchalantly slipped into her car and drove to a liquor store that was only four blocks away. The Jack Daniels helped me to get over the jittery effects of the crystal meth and I was feeling much better as we went back inside to watch Broken Bones. Before Broken Bones was too far into their set, my new companion gave me the "let's go somewhere quieter" sign.

Her band rented a permanent studio nearby that we could hang out at. The studio was less than 15 minutes away, still in downtown LA, and was a medium-sized, carpeted room with a drum set and musical equipment. As soon as the door was shut, there was no hesitation from either of us. It was as if we had known each other for a lot more than just three hours. After, when we were lying there naked on a soft rug right next to the drum set, she confessed that she had a boyfriend, and that he was the drummer of her own band. He had a key and he regularly came by the studio. She appeared to be getting turned on, as if the danger of her boyfriend possibly bursting in to catch us made her even hotter. I was too tired, too high, and too horny, to be concerned about her boyfriend. We decided not to worry about it and went about our business until it was daylight. She

Shaka Brah...Dude

was that special girl that put the punctuation mark on that special night at the end of a special tour. At 7 a.m. the next morning, she drove me to the band's pre-arranged meeting place near Melrose Place and we headed back to San Diego. The Broken Bones tour was officially over. The Northeast tour and the Broken Bones tour, which had brought us to San Diego from New York City, had been unqualified successes. Chris and George were happier and more motivated than ever, and I found myself in San Diego with a thousand dollars in my pocket, anchored into a band that I was thrilled to be in.

I had not planned on ending up in San Diego, and six months ago, if you had given me 50 guesses on where I'd be, San Diego would not have been one of the guesses. Fate just happened to bring me here. On the plus side, San Diego was spectacularly beautiful and the people remarkably polite. I was staying at my brother Isaac's nice, comfortable house in North County where he lived with his wife Debbie and two daughters, Faryn, who was almost five years old, and Harlye, who was three. Suffice to say that a 22-year-old punk rock drummer killing time until his next tour did not fit in with the suburban house with two kids and a dog lifestyle. I wouldn't trade the time I spent with my two young nieces for anything in the world, so I am grateful that they let me stay there for almost a month and a half, but any longer, and Debbie would have had a nervous breakdown or divorced my brother. It all worked out well in the end.

George and Chris were back home and doing their own thing with their girlfriends, so that left me by myself, deep in the hills of San Diego, with only the phone number of a random girl that I had briefly met at last week's party. I was truly concerned that I had been abandoned with nothing to do, and San Diego is no New York City, which at least had an accessible, active punk scene. James told me not to worry. He would introduce me to his

Shaka Brah...Dude

surfer friends, and he was sure that I would enjoy hanging out with them. He was right...the surfer dudes ruled, and they were a blast to hang out with! James took me down to Mission Beach and introduced me to all of his surfing buddies, and they took me in as one of their own. I became pals with the leader of the group, Tom, and we went to parties, saw bands, or just hung out and drank beer with the entire group. On the West Coast, it was fairly common that surfers were into punk rock. I'm not a surfer and was probably accepted into the group primarily because I was the drummer of Battalion of Saints, but that worked for me. These guys were super nice, morally sound, and always looking to have a fun time. I was a newcomer to this large city and only visiting for a short while and was grateful to have this awesome group of friends to hang out with.

Our next show was not till the end of February, which gave me plenty of time to get into some kind of trouble or another, which of course, I did. A pretty surfer girl named Janet had been flirting with me for a couple of weeks, and so I finally asked her out. I told Tom about our date, and Tom, after confirming it was the right Janet, informed me that she was the girlfriend of a local surfer named Big Jim. That should have been my warning sign. I had seen Big Jim around a few times, and everybody seemed to fear him, but Janet was a 5'3", dark-brown-haired, green-eyed surfer chick, with a lithe, surfer chick's body, and she had told me that she and Jim were currently broken up. Turns out, that wasn't completely true and she was just looking for somebody to make Jim jealous with, and I was an easy target. Saturday night, I left at her house the Kawasaki 400 motorcycle that I had recently bought for $400, and we drove in her VW Bug to El Torito Mexican Restaurant on Mira Mesa Blvd. in North County for dinner and lots of Margaritas. We hit it off very well. So well, that on the way back to her house, she pulled into the parking lot of a panoramic beach in Encinitas that was 20 yards away from

Shaka Brah...Dude

the Pacific Ocean. After she parked the VW, she got out and came over to the passenger side where I was sitting. Without saying a single word, she pulled down my pants and climbed right on. I offered no resistance. Man, did I love California!

A few days later, Tom called to let me know Jim was looking for me and that I should be careful. I called Janet to confront her about Jim and her answer was, "Well, we're **kind of** broken up, but maybe not really." She then asked if I wanted to go out with her again! I had no issue with Janet, as it was her choice to go out with whomever she wanted. Besides, she was hot, so I would just have to deal with Big Jim. But, I did tell her we were done.

The following Friday night, Battalion of Saints was booked at Ken Theatre in downtown San Diego. I always enjoyed playing live, so I was excited to play, and was not even contemplating that I might get my ass kicked that night. As the theatre began to fill, more than one of my surfer buds warned me that Big Jim was on the way and looking to fuck me up. Oh shit...I had no place to hide. I asked George and Chris for help, but Chris just shrugged his shoulders and walked out of the dressing room without saying a word. George was my last hope. George looked at me, cackled, and said, "You did fuck her, right?"

I said, "Yes."

"Then fucking deal with it then." Then he also walked out of the dressing room. Now I was worried. To occupy my mind, I started to make the final adjustments to my drum set. The converted movie theatre had an odd shape, and the box office was in plain view of where I was working on the drum set. And there appeared Jim. He was in line to buy a ticket at the box office, not to see the bands mind you, but solely to beat the crap out of me. He was looking at me with his fist clenched and

Shaka Brah...Dude

clearly mouthing, "I'm gonna fucking **kill** you," to me. He was saying it with a ferocious intensity that under different circumstances, I would have found comical, because he had to patiently wait his turn to buy a ticket while he was threatening me. I took that time to psyche myself up. I wasn't just going to roll over and let him pound on me. I was going to beat **him** up!

Finally, he got his ticket, handed it to the agent by the velvet rope, and ran towards me. I got from behind the drum set and took a few quick steps to meet him. I could tell it surprised him a little and I asked him roughly, "What the fuck is your problem?"

He seemed confused by my attitude, so he just answered me, "You fucked, Janet."

"Yes, I did! So what?" I dismissively answered.

"Well, she's my girlfriend!" he answered back with a little less conviction in his voice.

"She didn't tell me she had a boyfriend!" I shouted at him, as if I was the one who should be mad."

"She didn't?" he asked.

"Of course not! I wouldn't have gone out with her if I knew you were her boyfriend." I was being semi-honest, because technically, Tom had mentioned it to me. The right thing to do would have been to ask Jim directly before going out with her, but I kind of skipped that step. By the good grace of God, my aggressive tactic worked. Big Jim not only left me alone, but also carried all of my drum equipment onstage when it was time for Battalion of Saints to play. We remained friends and he even got back together with Janet. I loved California!

Shaka Brah...Dude

A week later on Sunday, March 3rd, I went with the whole surfer gang to The Rock Palace on El Cajon Blvd. to see Hüsker Dü, Minuteman, and The Meat Puppets. The day before, on Saturday afternoon, we had played a raucous game of softball that involved lots of beer, and I bone-headedly broke my wrist sliding into home plate. My hand swelled up to the size of a grapefruit, and so under an assumed name, I checked into the emergency room where X-rays confirmed that I had indeed fractured my wrist. The doctor offered to put me in a cast, but I declined because Battalion of Saints was due to start rehearsing in three weeks for a quickly approaching North American tour, so I had no time for a cast.

That night, right after Hüsker Dü finished playing, a big fight broke out between my surfer-dude friends and some out-of-town assholes, and I was in the middle of it, shoving guys around. When the altercation progressed beyond the shoving stage, I decided that even with my wrist fucked up, I was going to throw some punches. Tom saw me and told me that I needed my wrist to drum. You wouldn't ever think a surfer would say something so thoughtful, especially in the middle of a full-on, serious brawl, but these guys were like that. They truly had my back. Five seconds later, Tom was trying to disconnect a guy's head from his neck. Shaka brah, dude!

Meanwhile at home, my brother and I had come to the mutual conclusion that it would be better if I stayed Downtown with George and his mom. When George saw my swollen hand, he shook his head, "Will you be able to drum in three weeks?" I was 22 years old and felt like the Wolverine character from X-Men who heals instantly, so I told him not to worry. Three weeks later, we rehearsed for five straight days, and by the last day, I wasn't even thinking about my lame wrist anymore.

Shaka Brah...Dude

We had been in San Diego for two and a half months, and as fun and as cool as it had been, we were itching to get back on the road. This time the road would be just about every major city between San Diego and Montreal and then back again to California. It was 55 different cities in 90 days. The road dogs were back on the road…awooooo!

Battalion of Saints Do America

If our first night in Tucson was any indication of what the rest of the tour would be like, we were in for a wild fucking ride. We played inside of a large, opened up, high-ceilinged house that looked like The Addams Family mansion. The band set up at the front of the house, and the entrance to the show was at a bank of doors in the rear. As the room began to fill up, although not a lot of alcohol was consumed, it seemed as if people were still acting impaired. George, Chris, and Scarlet, now our tour manager, had each dropped a hit of acid, and were reporting that it was strong stuff. Before going on stage, James and I split a hit, and shortly after taking it, because Scarlet wasn't in any condition to handle anything, I was called on to sort out an issue with some kids who didn't want to pay to get in. I walked over to set those kids straight. No money, no show. But as the acid started to kick in, it seemed as if the right thing to do was to let those kids in for free, and so I did. It crossed my mind that the other kids waiting in line to pay might then insist on also getting in for free, but because of the effects of the acid, that no longer bothered me.

Although it hadn't occurred to me before, now that I had drunk from the same punch bowl as everyone else, I realized that the crowd was tripping, not drinking. Our performance that night was like a hardcore punk rock Grateful Dead show. It was weird, but there were no problems, no hassles, and since everybody was on the same wavelength, it turned out really well. I had taken the acid relatively late, so I didn't begin to peak until after we had finished playing.

Battalion of Saints Do America

Once I started peaking...oh man! It was like nothing I'd ever experienced. The posters on the walls came to life and I could see and hear the walls themselves breathing. Even in that condition, I attempted to appease a group of kids who had asked to buy some Battalion of Saints concert shirts. I grabbed the shirts that they wanted, but in my tripping state of mind, suddenly, I wanted nothing to do with money. I told them all that I was sorry but couldn't handle selling them anything right now. They were so nice about it and even told me that they understood where I was coming from! I ended up hanging out with one of the girls that wanted to buy a shirt...a sweet, pretty, U of Arizona student. We went outside, but when we started to make-out, it felt as if our bodies were melting into each other and that the large cacti all around us were turning into giant snakes and slithering on top of us. I stayed cool during it all but couldn't make the hallucinations stop. Finally, the girl offered to take me to her apartment, which sounded like a fabulous idea.

Two short blocks into the walk to her apartment we reached a small park, which in my eyes looked like a roaring jungle. After a couple of attempts at trying to cross it, I gave up. For some reason, I was afraid to walk through the park. Eventually, the girl shrugged her shoulders and left me to go home. The next morning, as I was walking to find a coffee shop, I saw that the park was tiny, maybe only ten yards wide, and that the dorm rooms were only one block past the park. I had fucked up! Left on my own, I returned back to The Addams Family Mansion, where the hallucinating phase of my trip was replaced by the laughing phase, whereby at five in the morning, as everyone was trying to get to sleep, I found calling our host Tina, Tuna, to be hilarious. Tina didn't appreciate the humor, and the guys in the band, not wanting any complications with our lodging arrangements, asked me to please leave until my trip had subsided. I didn't have a prayer of falling asleep so I located a

Battalion of Saints Do America

Dunkin' Donuts next to the college and drank plain, whole milk and ate donuts until I sobered up enough to go back to the house. Finally, I was able to fall asleep.

This was only our first night on the road. You might say that we were not exactly pacing ourselves. The next 21 days we played in 14 different cities: Albuquerque, Amarillo, Oklahoma City, Dallas, Austin, San Antonio, Houston, Baton Rouge, New Orleans, Tallahassee, Gainesville, Orlando, Tampa, and then down to Miami. The pattern was the same for every city that we played in. We would arrive, set up the equipment, do a sound check, hang out, play our show, and then end up at a party that was being held in our honor. It was a never-ending cycle. In every city, the guys all wanted to hang out with us, and the girls, well, also wanted to hang out with us! In Oklahoma City I witnessed two locals that mutually agreed to "step outside" and then beat the living shit out of each other. Even the party at the house we crashed at was marred by some intense violence, and I was still a little freaked out even after everybody had left. But as a consolation, one of the hot roommates let me crash in her bedroom while the rest of the band crashed in the living room. Even she was a tough Okie.

Our shows in Texas coincided with the Jewish holiday of Passover, which commemorates the exodus of the Jews out of Egypt. Instead of bread, for the eight days of Passover I ate only matzah, or unleavened bread. It's something you don't expect to see. A punk rock drummer touring through the debauchery that is Texas, eating matzah like a good Jewish boy. I'm not saying I'm a good Jewish boy, but for eight days, I did only eat matzah.

We spent two days in San Antonio drinking and partying at The Alamo with what seemed like a never-ending round robin of sexy rock and roll girls. I don't know where they even came from. It was as if they magically appeared. The concert in San Antonio, which was at a spectacular hall with large, overhanging balconies, was almost an afterthought.

In Houston, I met a girl in her mid-to-late-20's, who let Scarlet and me crash at her house. The next morning, on the way to giving us a ride back to the transport van, we picked up her six-year-old son at his grandmother's house to give him a ride to school. When he first got into the car, I was a bit shocked cause I was a 22-year-old kid myself. But after giving it some thought, the young MILF, well, technically MIDF, captured my respect. Just because she had a young son it didn't mean she couldn't live her life. When the boy looked at me with a glimmer of hope in his young eyes, I thought to myself, "Sorry son, I'm definitely not your new daddy." And we were gone. Before leaving Houston, the band bought some pharmaceutical MDMA pills. These were the pure, pharmaceutical grade precursors to what is now commonly known as Ecstasy or Molly. I decided to save mine for a special occasion.

Dallas topped them all. We played with the Circle Jerks, and more than 1,000 kids showed up for the show. After the concert, at the requisite party, I became friendly with one of the girls that was living in the house where the party was, and we ended up in her bedroom. While we were sitting on her bed, she told me that it was important that nobody find out about us because some people at the party were friends with her live-in boyfriend, who happened to be in Galveston surfing for the weekend. Her secret was safe with me, so it was game on! The Dallas surfer chick was assertive and strong, and while I was holding on for dear life, I saw the door to her room open wide and Scarlet standing in the doorway. There could be no misinterpreting what was going on in our room, which was now in view of the party. Scarlet mercifully closed the door after I yelled at him.

Battalion of Saints Do America

Casually, the girl then told me, "Oh, the lock on the door is broken." Now she was telling me? Undeterred, I said, "No problem," and pushed her full-size dresser in front of the door. A few minutes later, after we were back at it, Scarlet pushed the door open again and knocked the whole fucking dresser over with a super-loud crash! What was really cool about this girl was that she then said, "Everyone knows now anyway, so fuck it." I dutifully straightened up her dresser, and after Scarlet promised to finally leave us alone, stayed in her room until the next morning. I figured I would never see this girl again and so would never have to deal with the boyfriend, but that's not the way it turned out. The promoter was so happy with the turnout at his Dallas club that he offered us $3,500 to play again on the way back to the West Coast. Fuck…it was Big Jim all over again!

Our next set of shows through the South all had their share of excitement. In Baton Rouge I got my very first tattoo. It was a skeleton likeness of the drummer from the famous Revolutionary War picture, The Spirit of '76, designed and put on my bicep by the tattoo artist/stripper, Lady. After our concert at Tulane University we drank an excessive amount of Jägermeister. If you're familiar with Jägermeister, you're probably not surprised that Scarlet almost went through a storefront glass window that night. We played at Florida State University and University of Florida. In Orlando, there was a big fight between the ignorant fucking neo-Nazi skinheads and the punk rockers. We fought on the side of the punk rockers of course. Neo-Nazis represented a very small minority of the hardcore scene and were never welcome at any legitimate shows. By the third week in April we had made it all the way down to Miami, which was obviously something I was looking greatly forward to. It was now my turn to introduce my new band to the great music fans of South Florida. The show at

Battalion of Saints Do America

Flynn's on Miami Beach was amazing. I was proud of myself, my band, and proud of all my friends from South Florida.

The next day, the guys in the band all hung out at my parents' house while I took care of some personal stuff. The last two times I had been in South Florida, I had been forced to leave quickly. My father, who was leaving to go to work, asked if my mom was safe with these freaky, scary looking Battalion of Saints guys that were lounging around the house. My mother's answer, which seemed to satisfy my dad, was "I've never felt safer in my life." There comes a time in every parents' lives when they know their son or daughter is not coming back to them again. This was that moment.

The next morning we hit the road for the nine-hour drive to South Carolina to kick-off the next leg of the tour, which would take us all the way to Montreal and Toronto. It was Charleston, Columbia, Raleigh, Richmond, Virginia Beach, College Park, Baltimore, Georgetown, D.C., Harrisburg, Allentown, New York City, Atlantic City, Philadelphia, Asbury Park, Long Branch, New Haven, Montreal, Toronto, and Syracuse.

That's 20 cities in 25 days, which included only a 3-day break scheduled in Lake Placid, New York.

Maybe it was because we played near a lot of colleges, but the South was much more progressive than I thought it would be. We got our fair share of funny looks, but nobody gave us any real trouble. We had a few hours to kill before being interviewed at the University of South Carolina radio station in Columbia, so I decided to hang out in the student cafeteria, which was downstairs from the radio station. I ate by myself and just sat there observing the other kids in the cafeteria. They were all about the same age as me, and I wondered if I could do what they were doing. Like I've said all along, I fully appreciate what a college education could do to change someone's life, but my answer was still a resolute "no."

After playing in Charleston and Columbia, the next stop was The Brewery in Raleigh, North Carolina. This is the nightclub that Reed Mullins is standing in front of in the movie *American Hardcore* where he mentions Battalion of Saints playing there. Thank God he didn't mention Battalion of Saint's behavior, or more specifically, **my** behavior.

The opening band had a female bass player that I was totally smitten by. Female musicians are so uncommon in the punk rock world that when you see one who can play her instrument well and is hot, she becomes doubly desirable. This girl was smoking hot! After they finished playing, I complimented her on how well the band had sounded and how well she had played...you know, the usual standard pleasantries. After we played, she repaid the compliments back to me, and it was on from there! We hung out together and were getting along really great at the after-gig party, which was at the house where both of our bands would be staying that night. How convenient.

Early during the party, Scarlet decided that **we had to have** snakebites, which is malt liquor beer mixed with hard apple cider. The hot bass player and I volunteered to walk to the store and buy it, but the store, which was right across the street from North Carolina State University, didn't have hard apple cider. Instead, we bought Elephant Malt Liquor and champagne to mix it with, in place of the apple cider.

Oh boy! I did not handle the combination of malt liquor and champagne very well and got seriously intoxicated. At some point, understandably, the bass player left me to go hang out with her own band, who had all gone upstairs to a loft in the house. Politely, at first anyhow, I asked her to come down and continue hanging out with me. When she refused, I became obnoxiously belligerent and started throwing empty cans of beer up at everyone in the loft and threatening to "kick all of your asses." Anybody who knows me, knows that I'm a fun-loving, non-violent person. But they didn't know me, and based on my behavior, I seemed quite the opposite. As the night wore on, I got even more out of control and when Chris Smith egged me on into swinging the homeowner's guitar into the wall as if it were a baseball bat... "Joey Wrecked, up at the plate," he taunted. I did swing it, opening up a giant hole in the wall.

Mercifully, I eventually passed out in one of the rooms. When I woke up the next day, the owner of the house was with a friend who was holding a real baseball bat and following me around the house. I finally asked George, "George, why are these guys following me around with a baseball bat?"

"You mean you don't remember?"

"Remember what?"

"You put a hole in his wall with a guitar, asshole!"

It started coming back to me. I remembered swinging the guitar into the wall. Apart from not wanting to get bashed in the head with a bat, I felt bad about what I had done and wanted to make it right. They had asked George for $100 to fix the wall, but I offered to fix it myself. I drove the van to a hardware store, bought a piece of sheet rock and some plaster, and went back and patched the wall. We gave them $20 to paint the wall and they called it even. We were supposed to stay there that night, but they asked us to get the fuck out. When we stopped for breakfast on the way to Richmond, our next stop, the guys refused to let me sit at the table with them. My feelings were hurt, but I knew these guys loved me. Deep down I'm sure they were cracking up about my outrageous behavior.

We continued the tour by playing at the University of Maryland and at Georgetown. Disappointingly, our show at the 9:30 Club, which is an iconic venue to play at in Washington, D.C., was cancelled, so we had a few extra days to kill in the D.C. area.

That's when Scarlet did the deed to James Cooper, forcibly kicking him out of the band and taking over as the bass player. During the fight with Scarlet, one of James's boots had come off, and as James was running after the van with tears of fury in his eyes, Scarlet threw the boot at James's head. It was an ugly chapter in the Battalion of Saints story. As I already mentioned, James was immediately picked up by the highly respected band Meatmen to tour and record.

I was concerned about going back into CBGB, which was only a week away, with Scarlet on bass, because the NYC audience would be greatly disappointed if Battalion of Saints was anything less than our best. The show at CBGB, which was recorded and then later released on a CD in 2012, was nothing less than Battalion of Saints at our best. When you take into account that the faster tempos were designed to inspire a live audience and that the conditions inside of CBGB were far from the pristine conditions found inside of a recording studio, the results from the live recording are even more impressive.

In Atlantic City, we did a special show as the opening act for our friends from England, GBH, and a few days later, we were in Asbury Park headlining at one the most famous rock clubs in America: The Stone Pony. We were truly enjoying ourselves as a band and had even gotten our much-needed second wind. After putting in the miles to play our way up the coast to Montreal and Toronto, and then back down to Syracuse University, we were ready for our three-day vacation in Lake Placid. One of my major disappointments was that our show in Buffalo, that was supposed to follow Toronto, was cancelled at the last moment. I had made arrangements to see my steamy Canadian friend from the flight into Pittsburgh, in Buffalo. We had waited so long and now we would never see each other again.

In Lake Placid we relaxed, went trout fishing, and lived like humans in a gorgeous country house one of Chris's sisters owned. We were so out of touch with the normal way of doing things none of us could remember if the shower liner went inside or outside of the tub. We should have asked because the water that escaped from that upstairs bathroom as a result of having the shower liner on the outside of the tub, leaked all the way to the first floor. The much-needed long showers felt great, but we felt horrible about the water damage we caused.

During our break, we set up the musical equipment in the barn outside and worked on writing songs for the next album. Chris would start us off with a cool guitar riff, and Scarlet (who was now the bass player) and I would pitch in ideas about the changes and breaks, and collectively, we completed three new songs in their entirety. We had been listening to a lot of Iron Maiden and Judas Priest. The influence was clearly noticeable in the new songs, which we called New Songs #1, 2, and 3. The lyrics came out of a notebook that George always had with him to jot down ideas in. These were good, hard-driving songs, and two of the songs, renamed "Liar, Liar" and "Blue Eyed Devil" were scheduled to be released in late 2018 by Battalion of Saints.

Battalion of Saints Do America

After the break in Lake Placid, we were off to the Midwest to play 15 different cities in three weeks. The tour started in western Michigan, followed by Detroit, Cleveland, Columbus, and Pittsburgh, and then dipped into the south to Atlanta, Memphis, and Nashville, and then back up again to Urbana, Minneapolis, Kenosha, and Chicago and then all the way down to Dallas, finishing up in Kansas City and St. Louis. That's a lot of driving! Instead of a comfortable tour bus or planes and hotels, our mode of travel was a basic, 1973 Dodge van being held to the asphalt by the four $15 re-treaded tires that we had put on it in San Diego. In less than two months we had already played in 35 different cities and had driven more than 5,000 miles to do so. The next 21 days we would drive 3,000 miles to play in 15 more cities…awooooo!

You would think at this point we would have settled into a workman-like routine of playing our concerts and then conserving our energy by resting until it was time to play in the next city. Battalion of Saints just didn't roll that way. Every fucking city was a party and every fucking city was an adventure. The first show after our vacation in Lake Placid was in the suburbs of western Michigan, in Muskegon.

Before we get to Michigan, do you remember that MDMA pill that I bought in Houston? Well, I still had it with me while the band was in NYC. While I was there, I had spent the day with my ex-girlfriend Sonnie walking around St. Marks Place and enjoying a beautiful New York Saturday afternoon. In one of the trendy boutiques on St. Marks' Place, she eyed some cute leopard print panties that cost $25. We weren't spending $25 for a pair of panties! After we walked out of the boutique, I surprised her by reaching into my jeans and presenting her with the leopard panties I had just stolen for her. I know; how romantic. That same night, as we were hanging out at

Danceteria, Sonnie and I split the Ecstasy pill, and when it hit us, you might say that our relationship was rekindled. A few hours later I discovered firsthand that she was wearing the leopard panties that I had stolen for her.

We decided to get back together as boyfriend and girlfriend, but the next day, as I was leaving to go back on the road, Sonnie decided that she didn't want our relationship to officially start while I was still on the road because she knew what happened on the road. Thinking of it only through my eyes, I thought, "Great, I get a free pass for a month," so I agreed to her suggestion. Well, when I called her from a pay phone outside of a Harley dealer in Green Grass Fucking Western Michigan, I didn't expect that uncomfortable, "I can't talk right now," tone from her. WTF! I hadn't seen that coming! After we performed that night, I got hold of a bottle of Jack and chugged it till I heard yelled out of my mouth the words, "I want to pierce my balls!" Within seconds, George had whisked Chris, Scarlet and me into a bedroom and shut the door. He took off a stud earring from his own ear and asked me if I wanted him to do it.

"I'll do it myself," I snarled. I took a long hit from the Jack Daniels bottle and poked the semi-dull stud through my scrotum. As I was screaming from the pain, I held it in place as George put the backing on it. My balls hurt till we were all the way past Iowa more than a month later.

This was the first show in a long string of shows in the Midwest. The promoter would normally find us a place to stay for the night, usually in someone's house, but if he didn't, we were on our own. Since hotels were not in our budget, our strategy was for someone in the band to meet a girl and arrange for the rest of the band to stay there as well. In Cleveland I met a pretty, tall, thin brunette to go home with and arranged for Chris and

Battalion of Saints Do America

Scarlet to stay there as well. George was meeting up at a hotel room with his girlfriend, Janet, who was one of the financial backers of the band and had flown in from LA. Before George even dropped us off on the way to meet up with Janet, Chris had convinced the brunette to sleep with him instead of me. Motherfucker! I was pissed but was more tired than angry. When we got to the house, Scarlet and I were shown the basement, and Chris went inside with the pretty girl.

Twenty minutes later as we were falling asleep, Chris burst into the basement and said, "We have to get out of here right now!" He then quickly explained that the girl's mom had opened her daughter's door right when Chris's penis was smack dab in her mouth. Yep, future therapy issues for the mother and daughter aside, we now had no place to stay or access to transportation. The girl pointed us to a public park a few blocks away, supplied us with one blanket, and ran back into the house to deal with her hysterical mom. We found the park, and the three of us laid down on the bare grass with a blanket that didn't fully cover us. I purposefully pulled the blanket off Chris, who I was still pissed at, so that he was forced to lie there almost uncovered. Fuck him. We were so tired that we all had no trouble falling asleep.

But there's more. Around 6:30 in the morning, shortly after the sun came up, we were wakened by one of Cleveland, Ohio's finest police officers. We all thought we were going straight to jail for sure, but the pot-bellied officer told us not to worry, that we hadn't done anything wrong. He continued by telling us that he had received a report about three dead bodies in the park, and then showed us the Polaroid picture he had taken of us. It really did look like three corpses!

The next night, we uneventfully played at a club in Columbus a few blocks away from the University of Ohio and then headed east for the beautiful drive to Pittsburgh, which always rocked. Then, it was back down to Atlanta.

In Atlanta, we played at a beautiful concert hall called the Metroplex. Atlanta is a progressive, cool city, especially for the South, and playing in such a first-class venue for an appreciative crowd was enjoyable. Across the street from the Metroplex was an apartment loft well known for letting visiting bands and local kids alike, crash there for free. It was like a big hippie commune, but for punks, and that's where we spent the night. When I woke up, there was a cute local girl lying right next to me who had definitely crossed way into my personal space. There must have been 40 people in close proximity to us, but it was early, and since almost everybody was still asleep, I wanted to do more than just the touching that was now going on between me and the girl. When I whispered to my new bed neighbor what my plan was, she said no, and pointed to her boyfriend who was on a bed maybe 30 feet away from us. He could not have possibly known what we were doing under the sheets, but the guy was awake, and actually waved hello to us. Her hand was stroking my penis while the boyfriend was saying hi! Never one to over-contemplate the genesis of some of the situations that I sometimes found myself in, with the free hand that I wasn't rubbing his girlfriend with, I waved back. A few minutes later, the girl got up to lie with her boyfriend, and I slept like a baby.

At this rate, one of us was bound to be shot, incarcerated, or end up with an STD. I am happy to report that no bullets were fired, nor that anybody was thrown in jail. George was placed into handcuffs by police at the Double-O show at the 9:30 Club in D.C., but they let him go without booking him. Unfortunately, sometimes just looking like a punk was an arrestable offense in many cities. In Nashville, Scarlet began to complain that it was hurting him to pee. One day later, in Memphis, there was green discharge coming out of his penis, and he was in agony. The day after that, in Urbana, just outside of the University of Illinois where we played, we finally took him to a clinic. His cockney accent was so thick and unintelligible that it was necessary for me to go with him as an interpreter. Besides, I also wanted to get checked out. Sure enough, they had to Roto-Rooter Scarlet's penis, which is as painful as it sounds, with a round of penicillin to follow. I was given a clean bill of health. Party on, Garth!

We gobbled up the 500 miles of Wisconsin countryside between Urbana and Minneapolis till we got to First Avenue, the small alternative music club that is a part of Prince's spectacular First Avenue and 7th St. Entry nightclub, the setting for the movie *Purple Rain*. After our show, we stayed to see Morris Day and The Time at 7th St. Entry. The place was packed. Go figure. The next morning, we left the Land of 10,000 Lakes to arrive in Kenosha, Wisconsin, where we were treated to an industrial setting and a record amount of locally brewed beer. After playing the Kenosha show, Scarlet and I were so certain that the tough, mean looking guys that we were hanging out with were going to beat the shit out of us, that we devised an escape route **through** a house window. Scarlet was a big fucking guy and had worked security at clubs in London. That's how scary these guys were. Fighting them was just not an option. They ended up being super nice, and even let me fuck one of their girlfriends.

As a matter of fact, the beautiful blonde, the one I had sex with while her boyfriend was passed out in the next room over, drove 60 miles to be with me the next night in Chicago. She brought a friend with her that was equally as gorgeous! My plan however, was to hang out that night with my cousin Jack, who was a City of Chicago high school art teacher. Even cousin Jack was like, "Seriously dude, what are you even considering? I'll see you the next time." But that's not the way I roll. I set Jack up backstage at the spectacular Metro with food and liquor, and we hung out all night after the concert. I wouldn't have traded that night with my cousin Jack for those two beautiful girls, unless of course I had thought about it for just thirty seconds longer!

After Chicago, I had something more important to worry about. Next up, only 975 miles away, was Dallas. After sound check at the club in Dallas, the guys in the band made it clear that I was on my own to deal with the guy whose girlfriend I had banged in front of an entire room of people. So, as the crowd started to stream in, I waited all by my lonesome self for the certain impending, deserved, violent confrontation. This was a gigantic space, so there existed the possibility that he might not even see me. It was not to be. The two of them were walking together and headed right towards me. The girl gave me an almost imperceptible glance as I stood frozen like a deer, and then they walked right past me, almost bumping in to me as they did. The dude didn't know who I was! I was off the hook, again.

The Dallas show went well, and if possible, the after-party was even wilder than the last time. A gorgeous, half Filipina looking girl told me she was a close friend of the girl I had been with the last time, and with not many more words exchanged than that, took me into a room and took up where the other girl had left off. No exaggeration. I didn't speak ten words to this girl the entire time we were together. Fucking Dallas…I loved it! Five days later, we finished off that leg of the tour by playing on back-to-back nights on June 17th in St. Louis at Mississippi Nights and on June 18th in Kansas City at Fool Killer. In Kansas, George was almost duped into going with an underage girl, and was even tempted **after** he found out, but he ended up doing the right thing by sending the girl on her way. Some guy, whose feathers were ruffled by George's behavior, asked George to step outside to fight, and George agreed to it. When they both got to the front door, George stepped aside to let the man go through first. I happened to be standing only a few feet away as I was shadowing George and heard him say thank you to George's civil gesture. And that's when George grabbed the guy's head and ferociously slammed it against the hard door, knocking him completely unconscious. George laughed, mumbled something to me about the guy being an idiot, and then went back to his underage girl. In St. Louis, Chris had to punch a guy in the face who was mad because Chris was flirting with the guy's wife at the bar. It was a one punch and done affair also.

Minor skirmishes behind us, the next night we were booked to play in Iowa City, near the University of Iowa. Iowa would be the gateway to the final leg of our tour, which would culminate with some massive shows in the West that we wanted to get to already. The band was clearly exhausted, and we weren't looking forward to playing in Iowa. Sure enough, Iowa was where we faced the most serious challenge of the entire tour.

The Cornfields of Iowa and the Insane Asylum

There's nothing I won't do to help my band, so when the engine of the old Dodge van seized up on I-80 just past Des Moines, an hour and a half away from our gig in Iowa City, I volunteered to run through the cornfields to get help. We could see a building far in the distance through the cornfields that would surely have a phone to call the promoter, so that's where I headed. It felt strange running the mile and a half or so through the cornfields. It's not something most people ever do. When I got to the building, I was spooked even more. It was a huge sanitarium for people with mental health problems, and when I knocked on the doors, nobody opened them for me. I walked along the side of the building until I found a door that was unlocked and walked in. I asked an employee, who was wearing a starched white uniform and nurse's hat, if there was a phone I could use, but she didn't even answer me. This place was eerie, and I was unabashedly scared. Nobody in the band was capable of running that far through a cornfield to save me, and, if they finally came and couldn't find me, then what? No joke. I was on my own and terrified by this crazy place. I spotted a phone, and although a robotic sounding sanitarium employee started to object to my use of it, which was the first time that anybody in the building had even acknowledged my presence, I quickly called the promoter to let him know that we were broken down so he could come get us. He told me to sit tight and wait for him. I bolted out of the same door I came in from and ran back the entire way back to the van at an elevated pace. The combination of the creepy cornfield and the bizarre sanitarium had me more than just a little freaked out. The bad juju continued when we

The Cornfields of Iowa and the Insane Asylum

arrived three and a half hours later to Iowa City. There had been a bad fight between the jocks from the University and the punks at the club, which the punks had lost. We played for whoever remained at the club, but nobody in the band, or in the audience for that matter, was into it. Immediately after, we packed up our stuff so we could get back to our own van, which had now been towed to a gas station in Newton. And that's where we spent the night. In the van, at the gas station, in Newton fucking Iowa.

The next morning, the prognosis on the van came as no surprise. The pistons had seized, and the engine needed to be rebuilt, which cost around $1,700. Since we didn't have that kind of money, George had to call Janet in Los Angeles to ask her to send us cash. That's when the business end of the band started to fall apart. Janet and the other financial backers assumed that we had a lot more money from door receipts and T-shirt sales than we really had, and accused the band, or more specifically Chris and George, of wasting the band money on drugs. I can tell you that it was true that they bought some drugs. George and Chris certainly had a bit of a sweet tooth. But as far as I could tell, they hadn't gone overboard. More likely, the real issue was that Janet had found out about a girlfriend that George had in DC. If you believe Chris, she found out because George mistakenly turned in a hotel receipt with the girl's name on it, or, if you believe George, Chris outright tattle-tailed on him. Either way, we weren't getting any money. The band only had about $900 in cash, and the mood the entire next day was glum.

That night we splurged on a Midwestern-beef steak dinner that was dee-licious, and Chris and Scarlet decided to trip on some Iowa acid that was so powerful that I felt as if I was getting a contact buzz from just being near them. At first I thought, "We're broke. Why are we spending money on a steak dinner, and how could you guys trip at a time like this?" And then

The Cornfields of Iowa and the Insane Asylum

realized that's exactly what we needed. After dinner, we went back to the van and were listening to Metallica on the cassette player, when right in front of our eyes, a caravan of cars and motorcycles, probably 15 vehicles in total, arrived to circle the gas station over and over. The caravan drivers and passengers were yelling really imaginative, disparaging words such as "freaks" and "faggots." We grabbed whatever could be used as a weapon and prepared to storm them if they got out of their vehicles, which they never did. We would see that same caravan again the next day. Welcome to Newton fucking Iowa!

George and Chris had decided to give up and were shutting down the rest of the tour. Not on my watch!

The next morning I woke up with the intention of resolving our transportation issues and getting back on the road. I don't give up very easily and happened to be a bona-fide expert in dealing with broken down, shitty cars and making them work. I built my first bicycle when I was nine years old from discarded spare parts and used it for years after. While George, Chris, and Scarlet moped around, I asked the owner of the garage to take me to the used car/scrap lot that he also owned, which was only two miles away from the garage. Once there, he started hawking the "normal" used cars to me until it finally sunk in that I was looking to spend only about $500. He huffed deeply and then took me to the scrap side of his lot.

I looked around and saw a car that interested me.

"Does that yellow Chevy Malibu start?" I asked. "Is it a '69?"

"It's actually a '68," he responded with a more serious tone than I had so far been accorded. Something must have woken up

The Cornfields of Iowa and the Insane Asylum

inside of him. As if he had experienced a revelation, he then said, "That would be a good car for you."

"How much?"

"$600."

"I'll give you $400 for it."

"Make it $500, and I'll even sell you an old wooden trailer to haul your equipment for $150. The U-Haul store will attach a hitch on your car for $75."

The math worked perfectly for our situation. I said "Deal," and handed him the $650 in cash.

Once he saw that we weren't some trouble-making fuckups, this guy turned into a stand-up guy who sincerely wanted to help, and immeasurably did. He was embarrassed at the behavior of the local young folks that were acting like imbeciles, and even gave us $100 for the broken-down Dodge van that we were going to leave him anyway.

The very next day, the hitch was installed and the trailer was attached and loaded with all of our equipment, and we were off to Salt Lake City 1,100 miles away, in our fully functional, yellow, 1968 Chevrolet Malibu. The band was happy again. Very happy. The six cities that remained on our 55-city tour were Salt Lake City, Seattle, Portland, Sacramento, San Jose, and San Francisco. The $500 car would have to survive 2,900 miles through the mountains and along the Pacific Coast. If the car lasted that long, this would be the best $725 ever spent …awooooo!

Hello West Coast...Goodbye

We drove straight through the flatlands of Nebraska and Wyoming and arrived for our show in Salt Lake City with only a few hours to spare. There is a lot of empty space in Nebraska and Wyoming. The venue was an outdoor county fair, and the surprisingly large throng of punk rockers that were there to see us on this Saturday night were vastly outnumbered by the even larger numbers of "regular" people who stretched to the back of the fair grounds. It seemed really fucking strange to see three or four hundred punks enjoying our show right alongside such a mainstream audience. The world as we knew it just didn't work that way. Not that we gave a shit, but given the conservative religious reputation that Salt Lake City has, we were wondering how our brand of music would be received here. When we finished, the polite people of Salt Lake City gave us a warm reception. After the show, we ran into some people that ummm...weren't quite as polite.

As per usual, after our show we went to the house where we would be crashing for the night, which also as per usual, was the party house. I was as exhausted as I'd ever felt in my life, and after a short while at the party, went back to the Malibu to lie in the back seat and get some rest. Scarlet, who was always full of energy and never one to miss a good party, also confessed to being drained, and joined me in the car to lie in the front, bench-style seat. The car, with the trailer and all of our equipment, was on a sprawling, neglected, weed infested, concrete parking lot that was about half the size of a football field. We were parked near the far end, maybe 40 yards away from the house. I fell

Hello West Coast...Goodbye

asleep immediately but was awoken 20 minutes later by the sound of Scarlet and three other guys arguing loudly. The three guys had been offended because two, wild, blonde Mormon sisters had initiated a threesome with Chris Smith at the party.

The three guys, not expecting to find Scarlet and me in the car, had come to steal or vandalize our equipment. I stepped outside to try and calm things down but was promptly attacked by two of the guys. Acting solely on instinct, I grabbed the first guy that came at me and quite easily threw him to the ground and then pivoted and punched the second guy squarely in the face, which literally stopped him in his tracks. These two guys were tall, pencil-thin, low-life delinquents. The third guy was a completely different breed of criminal. He was a 6–foot-tall, 30-year-old, 250-pound Samoan dude, and he stepped in front of me as if to say, "Try that on me bitch!" Fuck that. I wasn't getting annihilated by this beast for something that Chris had done. Scarlet, who had quickly gone off to get some help, was now heading back my way with George in tow. In order to stall, I reasoned with the Samoan that his issue wasn't with me, which caused him to pause long enough for Scarlet, George, and a few other guys to get there. The three troublemakers turned and ran away, but I heard one of the skinny kids say he was going to get his gun. That's when I realized the situation might be serious. We were by ourselves in a semi-secluded area, so we hustled back to the house. Apparently, ours had not been the only conflict, and the house was now nearly deserted. As Scarlet and I were trying to figure out exactly what was going on and how to deal with it, Chris spilled into the house from the opposite direction as the parking lot.

"Where's George?" he asked in a panic.

Hello West Coast...Goodbye

The situation was so hectic, that Scarlet and I had no idea where George had wandered off to.

"We need to go get him!" Chris implored.

At the exact moment the three of us made it out the door and onto the porch, we heard a crashing noise and George screaming in sheer agony. He was only a few feet away, on the other side of some thick bushes, bleeding from his head and in horrific pain. He had been hit with a steel pipe that had dislocated his clavicle, punched, kicked, and had a beer bottle smashed on his head. So much for the polite people of Salt Lake City.

At the hospital, George's shoulder was put back into place and the pieces of glass removed from his head. There was a guy from the party who had been knifed in the abdomen pretty badly. The 10-inch gash looked gnarly, but thankfully, it was only superficial and he was going to be fine. Chris had done nothing to cause the senseless violence unleashed that night. Was he supposed to say no to the beautiful, blonde sisters? When I left the party, those girls had been all over him. Now George was in an extreme amount of pain as a result. After he was discharged from the hospital, it took some convincing to get him back in the car to head for our next show, which was in Seattle. He stayed absolutely silent during the 14-hour car ride through the lush green mountains of Washington State.

Like all frontmen, George enjoyed performing for an appreciative audience. Seattle, as everyone knows, is a great city for alternative music, and after seeing the super hip theatre that we were playing at, which was full to capacity, George felt a little more motivated to sing. The show in Seattle was very cool, and we got through it fine considering our scattered mindsets.

Hello West Coast...Goodbye

The next day we were off to Portland.

Just 15 minutes away from the Oregon border, I was pulled over by the Washington Sate Police and given tickets for speeding and for not having a special Washington State permit for our trailer. The no-nonsense officer told me that if he saw me driving again and I didn't have the permit, he was hauling me off to jail. Ain't **that** a fucking Catch-22? I needed the car to get the permit, but I needed the permit to use the car. We waited for five minutes and then I pulled back on the highway.

Portland had a really nice, small town sort of feel to it, and a mellower vibe than Seattle. There's no rhyme or reason for this, but all of a sudden, everyone in the band, including George, was in a good mood and re-energized. The club we were playing at was super-cool, and the sound system and sound crew were top-notch. We already knew it was going to be a good show, and it was. Afterwards, I was excited to see my friend Larry Lee, the bass player from Crank, who was now back in Portland. But I didn't spend too much time catching-up with him. Earlier in the evening I had met a cute, Goth-looking girl, who informed me upfront that she was a lesbian. I told her that was great...what else was I going to say? I kind of dug her, so I hung out with her. Before long, she told me that she liked the way I had handled what she told me and asked me if I wanted to go home with her. Turns out she was only a part-time lesbian. She had a dark, sharp angle to her, which I really liked. Before I left with her, I confessed to George that I had a faraway suspicion that this girl was going to stab me to death after I fell asleep. George's sage, sarcastic advice was, "Sleep with one eye open." He was in a good mood and we were buddies again, so he gave me one of the strong narcotic pills he was given at the ER in Salt Lake City, which I popped before leaving the club.

Hello West Coast...Goodbye

The Goth girl's apartment was decorated kind of like a spider's web and lit with a black light, which combined with the effects from the narcotics pill, created a dark, sexy ambience. We hung out all night listening to Alice Cooper records and let's just say that if this girl really was a lesbian, she did a great job of faking it with me. I put off from sleeping long as possible until I passed out at around five in the morning. The Goth chick had been a lot of fun, and she didn't stab me with a set of scissors as I slept!

Battalion of Saints was now headed to the spectacular Crest Theatre in Sacramento, California to co-headline with Social Distortion. What an epic show it was! We opened for them in Sacramento and they opened for us less than a week later at the historical San Francisco punk venue, The Farm. Sandwiched between the two Social Distortion shows, we headlined on our own in San Jose to a crowd of over 1,000 punk rockers. In San Francisco, Social Distortion bitched and moaned about opening for us. James Hetfield and Lars Ulrich, from Metallica, were reportedly hanging out with them backstage, and it was a capacity crowd. Social Distortion has now sold over 4 million records, but back then, they were just another mid-tier band, just as we were. So fuck them. Since we were both co-headlining, we insisted they play before us, which they begrudgingly obliged to. These three, exciting, larger-than-life shows were the perfect ending to our fifty-five city tour.

It had been the best three months of my life. If I could choose one thing to do for the rest of my life, this would be it. I loved playing good music each night in a different city to an appreciative audience, and I loved the perks that went with it. But I was frazzled to the bone and happy that this tour was now over. I needed a break, and I needed to assess my life. I was 22 years old, and possibly un-like most 22-year-olds, I was always thinking about my future. Each decision that I made, and the

Hello West Coast...Goodbye

outcomes of those decisions, would stay with me for a long time. Only a few years ago I had decided to drive a stolen car across the state of Florida to a Black Flag gig. What if I had been caught? Do you think that would have affected my life significantly? Of course it would have. What about unloading two tons of pot? Before agreeing to do it, I thought about it for a full week beforehand, and then overwhelmingly decided that if I succeeded, that meant having the money to go to New York, which ended up basically being the portal to the rest of my entire life. Getting busted would have ushered in a completely different set of ramifications. What if I hadn't taken any risk at all? What then? Who knows where I'd be now. And that my friends, is what this life is all about.

It was 4th of July weekend, and Sonnie flew in to join me in San Francisco. I had already decided to fly back to New York with her before plotting my next move, which as of now, I had no idea of. We spent 4th of July at Golden Gate Park with my long-time buddy from back in South Florida, David Labrava (Happy, from the TV show *Sons of Anarchy*) and with some of George's friends from the Mission District. Also, with us was a girl from Walnut Creek who I had become very friendly with while visiting David earlier in the year. The yellow Malibu? The tour saving 1968 yellow Malibu performed like a hero, but the brakes were completely shot, and instead of fixing them, we just abandoned the poor car in San Francisco. The next morning, on Friday, George, Chris, and Scarlet left for San Diego with my pretty friend from Walnut Creek, who volunteered to give the band, and all of our equipment, a ride back to San Diego. Sonnie and I enjoyed being tourists in San Francisco and both of us got tattoos at Lyle Tuttle Tattoo on Market Street, where David Labrava worked at. Sonnie had a beautifully done, colorful dragon put on her by the legendary tattoo artist, Lyle Tuttle and Erno, Lyle's protégé, added a battle scene as a background to my

Hello West Coast...Goodbye

Spirit of '76 drummer. Sunday we dropped off the $16.95 per-day rental car at San Francisco Airport and we boarded a plane to New York City. I had no idea what was next for me, but at the moment, I felt really, really good. I was proud of how successful the tour with Battalion of Saints had been, and I was excited to be heading back to New York City. The future was wide open.

Take Me Back to New York City

One week after the tour ended, three of the four members of Battalion of Saints, Chris, Scarlet, and me, met in NYC to discuss our plans. I had moved in with Sonnie and Rose into their one-bedroom apartment on Mulberry Street, Scarlet had stopped off in New York on the way to returning to London, and Chris Smith had officially moved to New York City to be with his girlfriend and near his family. Chris immediately announced that he was done with Battalion of Saints. Between the constant financial bickering of the shareholders (Battalion of Saints was incorporated and had shareholders) and the backstabbing between Chris and George, it didn't make sense for me or Scarlet to remain in the band either. If Chris was out, then Scarlet and I were out as well. It was that simple, and our meeting ended quickly. Although George was disappointed with my choice, he was, and still is, a true friend, and supported my decision to do what I thought was best for me. George Flores Anthony was the founder of the band and planned to continue on with Battalion of Saints with or without us. Keeping Battalion of Saints alive meant that one of the very finest of the old school American punk bands would live on. But I wouldn't be a part of it.

Quitting the band? You have to be thinking, "Really?" After describing my time with Battalion of Saints as "The wildest and most fun time of my life," and stating that, "If I could choose one thing to do for the rest of my life, this would be it," and then just like that, see ya? How could that be? It's simple. Since high school, every step that I took and every band and band member that I chose to play with was thought through. Once I decided to commit, right or wrong, smart or idiotic, it was 100%. I always looked to be in a band that had great songs, sounded great playing them, and had a unique chemistry the public would find themselves drawn to. With the goal of getting signed to a major record label always in mind, I did what was necessary to put myself in the position for that. As much as I loved George and the music of Battalion of Saints, it was time for me to move on.

What was next in the glamorous world of rock and roll? Nothing! I went to work with Chris at a roach coach lunch wagon business that his brother owned in Little Falls, New Jersey. It was a 40-minute bus ride each day from Port Authority in New York City, followed by eight hours of loading lunch wagons with chemically laced, bland food and keeping the tanks fueled with propane. I was grateful for the work because I needed the money to pay for my share of the rent, but fuck if I was going to stock lunch wagons for the rest of my life.

It was time to go back to college again. But man, those out-of-state tuition fees were a fortune. Who could afford this shit? I needed to not only transition from being a hardcore road dog into a civilized, knowledge embracing student, but to also figure out how to pay for it. My father offered to help pay for the cost of school, and although I appreciated the offer, felt that at almost 23 years old, I shouldn't remain a financial burden on my parents. This had to be done on my own. It occurred to me that the in-state rates at Baruch College were considerably cheaper than the out-of-state rates, and based on my financials, I'd easily qualify for financial assistance. So that became my plan of attack.

I had been off the grid for a few years, so if I suddenly appeared as a permanent resident of New York State, who would be able to question it? Exactly. I went to the Post Office and picked up some IRS tax forms and filed Federal and NY State tax returns, listing myself as a permanent resident of New York State. I made copies of those returns and then marched into the Admissions office and applied to City College of New York (Baruch College), as a New York resident. A few weeks later, after my transcripts from Florida had been received and processed, I was admitted to Baruch College by the admission's office as an in-state resident. The Office of the Registrar tried to disallow the transfer of 24 of my 62 credits from Florida, but at the entrance interview, I was able to convince the guidance counselor, who seemed to be clearly flirting with me, to bring it down to eight credits. I smiled at her while I pleaded my case, and just like that, with a stroke of her pen, she saved me almost a year of classes. My, I'm-in-the-band, charm was clearly still intact. My next appointment was with the financial aid officer.

After being on the road for so long, I was at a minimum, a little rough around the edges. Sal Ferrante, the financial aid officer at Baruch College, was probably just doing his job by questioning the validity of my application. At the beginning of the interview, I amicably answered all of his questions. He was looking over my tax returns and didn't seem to believe that it was possible for someone to survive in New York City on the small amount of income that I was claiming to have earned. If he was asking for an explanation, I was happy to provide it, and I did. I patiently explained that surviving with very little money was not easy, but it was certainly possible, and that plenty of people in the city got by with very little. I had slept more than once in abandoned buildings in the Lower East Side. It was called squatting, and although it was Spartan at best, it was free. I could certainly understand his pessimism, but when he insinuated I was lying, my temper quickly spiraled out of control, and despite efforts to curb it, my rage overtook my intellectual sensibilities.

Take Me Back to New York City

I was no longer in a hallowed, civil, university setting, but rather, back in the streets with my survival at stake. With my eyes flashing like lightning bolts, in a gravelly, low-volume growl, I asked Mr. Ferrante to step outside with me. I didn't mind a good-faith interview, but if he was going to insult me, he was going to pay a price. Sal Ferrante was a robust, tough looking, hard-nosed guy, and my full expectation was that he would do exactly as I had requested, which was to go outside and fight me. What he did next, however, has stayed with me forever. He completely changed. He changed the way he was talking to me and he changed what we were talking about. Mr. Ferrante was neither afraid nor intimidated by me. He simply realized at that moment that I was telling the truth, and not only wanted to help me, but was instantly attune to the delicate nature of my particular set of circumstances. If he would have made it difficult for me to attend Baruch College, my happy ending story might have had an all-together different, not so happy ending. Think about it. How many people would try and help someone that has just threatened them? How many people would have called security to escort me out or have used their position of power to dole out punishment? Sal Ferrante was not an insecure bully, but rather, a dedicated, higher-education professional. Thank God for that. He never gave me any preferential treatment, but he did make sure that I received all the financial assistance that I qualified for.

When fall classes began in September, I was signed up for a full schedule of classes. The transition from touring with Battalion of Saints to just another student attending classes at college took less than two months. Almost overnight, I went from sex, drugs, violence, fun, and rock and roll to marketing, political science, finance, statistics, et bien sûr, French. It's not as radical as it sounds. At almost 23 years old now, I was old enough to think ahead and do what was best for me, but still young enough to change my life on a dime. Finishing my college degree was the right thing to do, and this was the right time to do it. And so, when school began, I went to class, learned the material, and passed my exams. I wasn't in college to fuck around or drop classes or fail exams and even maintained a GPA that for a while placed me on the Dean's List. Some of the required classes were kind of bullshit, but most of the courses unveiled a secret world that only people who go to college ever get to find out about. By the time I graduated, I had studied chemistry, micro and macro economics, international finance, history, calculus, regression analysis, statistics, marketing, corporate management, investment management, political science, philosophy, and much more, and of course, was now practically fluent in French.

For almost two years, I worked for six hours a day at a construction job split between Staten Island and Brooklyn and went to school full time. Some days I took classes in the morning, worked the rest of the day, and then went directly back to school at night covered in dust and wearing my construction boots. What was cool about Baruch College was that nobody blinked at my hellish appearance. All of the students were there for an education, not for the make-believe college experience. On the nights that I had no classes, I worked as the drum tech at Giant Studios, which was where all of the musicians that I knew rehearsed and jammed. Don't tell Fred, the owner of Giant Studios, but he was basically paying me to practice drumming. Obviously, I did not believe my music career was over yet.

If you listen to "Buddies and Pals" or "I Want To Make You Scream" by Battalion of Saints, you may not like it at first. That's OK, because I know that if you listen to Beethoven's 9th Symphony or anything by Charlie Parker or Buddy Guy, you might not like that either. That doesn't make them any less essential or any less magnificent. Most of us will rationalize that,

Take Me Back to New York City

"I just don't like that type of music." The forces that have been conditioning you to not like anything other than what is fed to you are happy that they have succeeded in limiting your tastes. More control, and more profit, for them. To a guy like me, who loves…better said, lives and dies by great music, it is shameful. Great music changes people's lives. I can't even imagine what this world would be like without great music. Could you?

Circus of Power

I happened to have been there for the punk rock movement of the late 1970's and early 1980's; the Sex Pistols, The Clash, The Ramones, Buzzcocks, The Jam, Stiff Little Fingers, Generation X, and many, many others. That was the creative and energetic music that touched my soul and that's why I played with The Reactions and Battalion of Saints. But all along, rock and roll was the blood my heart pumped throughout my body. I have listened to "Angie" by The Rolling Stones a hundred times. It tears me apart every time. That's what rock and roll is **supposed** to do. And so, in early October of 1986, I asked Ricky Beck Mahler if he wanted to start a rock band with me. His answer was, "Yeah, let's do that." Those four words were the start of Circus of Power. Alex Mitchel was the natural choice for singer and my good friend Rodrigo Schiffino, Gigo as he was called, volunteered for bass. Alex and Ricky were friends with a bartender in Tribeca named Bobby, who had interesting song ideas and a unique rhythm and blues type of sound. He also brought along a stubborn heroin habit. The first five members of the band that became known as Circus of Power met at the apartment I now shared with my ex-Battalion of Saints guitar player, Chris Smith, on 6th Street between Avenues B and C, east of Tompkins Square Park in Manhattan's Lower East Side.

We immediately got to working on our original songs, and by the end of November, we had eight good ones. With the addition of a few tasteful covers, like Del Shannon's "Runaway," we played our first show in Manhattan. It was at WGAF (Who Gives a Fuck) on E. 12th Street and 2nd Avenue. The people that came

Circus of Power

to see us were mostly our friends, so it wasn't a particularly large crowd, but there was no denying that our sound was original and that we had potential. For that show we were billed as The Strangers. For months afterwards, we tried to think of a new name for the band, but nobody could come up with anything that stuck. Finally, in early 1987, after work one day, I found Alex waiting for me in the hallway outside the door to my apartment, which was now back on Mulberry Street again. Alex had come up with a great new name for the band and wanted to tell me in person. With that faraway look that we sometimes see in mad scientists, he said to me, "Circus of Power should be the name of the band. What do you think?"

"I like it," I said.

Alex didn't even come into the apartment. He had said what he came there to say and then spun on his heels to go back to his own apartment across the street. I closed the door and repeated it to myself slowly, so as to hear it out loud, "Circus of Power."

What a great fucking name for our band!

Our sound was sleazy, ballsy, Southern tinged rock and roll, and our appearance was all of those things, with dirty outlaw biker thrown in. It wasn't an act. It was who we really were. As the band progressed, it became apparent that we needed to make some personnel changes. Both Gigo and Bobby left on good terms and were replaced by Gary Sunshine on bass at first, and then when Zowie eventually joined as the bass player, Gary moved to second guitar. Zowie and Gary were rock solid and were a big part of the reason for the band's success. Armed now with an entire set of powerful originals, with Ricky on lead guitar, Alex coming in to his own as a singer and a frontman, and my complimentary drumming, we quickly climbed to the

Circus of Power

top of the New York rock and roll scene. It was fast track all over again, but this time, the market was not underground punk rock, but rather, the infinitely larger rock and roll mass market. We were eyeing the same audiences as Guns N' Roses and Bon Jovi.

I remained grounded while all this new excitement was developing. I had a lot on my plate; a full schedule at college, a construction job, and now a band that had taken off remarkably quickly. I needed to make some changes and streamline my life if I was going to handle it all. I left Chris and his junkie girlfriend and moved in with Ricky on 12th Street between Avenues C and D. This was even deeper into the dangerous and crime rampant Lower East Side, and my accommodations were a convertible futon couch in the middle of the living room. The tenant on the lease was a good friend named Alice, who was the head bartender at the best club at the time in New York City, the legendary Danceteria. Madonna was a regular at Danceteria, and Ricky and I were permanently hooked up to get past the red velvet rope with no wait and drink for free. Nice perks, huh? It became necessary to move in with Alice and Ricky because the drama unfolding in the apartment with Chris and his girlfriend was making it difficult, if not impossible, for me to study for classes. Chris was madly in love with his girlfriend, Shannon, and even had her image tattooed on his arm in two different places. At the end of 1986, Shannon, who was still living in the same apartment as Chris, began dating another guy, who looked like a shorter version of Robin Zander from Cheap Trick. Chris handled it as well as possible, but I had to get the hell out of that apartment! Two months after I moved out, just as the winter 1987 semester was starting for me at Baruch College, Chris was found dead in the bathtub of his apartment. Although there were syringes strewn about, the circumstances surrounding his death remain very suspicious. I was told that he hit his head on the bathtub faucet and drowned, but the autopsy didn't find any water in his lungs. It was easy to look at the syringes and drugs and quickly come to the conclusion that he was just another junkie who overdosed, and so no further investigation was conducted. We'll never know what really happened the night he died. Another great guitar player, one of the best in the country, dead. When he died, he was playing guitar for his good buddy Davey Gunner's band, the inimitable Kraut. Even more exciting, only known by his closest friends, Chris was also recording lead guitar tracks for the band Samhain, a band whose reincarnations and past line-ups have sold many millions of records. When Chris Smith passed away, the world lost an artist who, without any shadow of a doubt, would have continued to significantly contribute to the music world. He was a very good friend of mine, and I still miss him badly.

I consciously decided that the passing of Chris would not affect my focus. There was too much going on, and too much at stake. I left my job working construction for Steven and Susan Agin in Staten Island to go work at Bond Gallery in Manhattan. Bond Gallery, on Bond Street, was close to my apartment, and not only was the pay better, but it was also interesting to be around all of the personable artists and entertaining characters involved with the art gallery. The owner, Bob, liked having me around as well, because aside from being able to do all of the work required, I fit in well with the eclectic scene there.

I was also no longer working at Giant Studios but was nevertheless still there almost every night rehearsing with the band. When it was time to record our demo, we caught a lucky break when a local named Donny offered to record us at his Downtown studio for only $500. He had previously hired Ricky and I to do some session work at his studio, and out of the kindness of his heart, wanted to help us out with our demo. We

Circus of Power

recorded "Letters Home," "Needles," "Turn up the Jams," and "Dreams Tonight", four of our strongest, catchiest songs.

As 1987 rolled by, I was a long-haired, rocking and rolling college student working at a super-hip art gallery. Circus of Power was killing it with weekly live shows at The Lismar Lounge in the East Village. The downtown Manhattan rock scene was exploding in popularity, and many of the bands from the scene, including our friends Raging Slab and Cycle Sluts from Hell, scored major record deals. Circus of Power was widely considered by most to be the leaders of the pack, so to say that I was loving life wouldn't even have begun to describe it. I was fucking floating. Even at school I was hitting my stride. The upper level courses that I was now taking were interesting, and I found myself becoming friendly with almost all of my professors, which was very different than when I first started at Baruch, when I felt totally alienated. The professors all knew me now and seemed genuinely interested in my progress. After the current semester finished in June, I would be left with only six credits remaining to graduate with a bachelor's degree. This was everything I could have asked for.

But this is where the story takes a very unexpected turn. Alex Mitchel committed to having us play at our ex-band member Bobby's Tribeca bar. I vehemently opposed it and argued that we were way past playing those types of places. We should be looking to play at bigger venues, and not at a local Tribeca bar. Alex insisted that he had made a commitment and that we should honor it. Ricky and I looked at each other dubiously, but to keep the peace, we agreed to do it. At 10 p.m. on the night of the gig, there was no sign of Alex, so we told Bobby we would go on at 11. When 11 came and went with still no sign of Alex, we took the stage without him and played 45 minutes of uninspired blues. The audience tried to be good-natured about it, but we were mortified. We had agreed to play this show solely to appease Alex, and then Alex didn't even show up? Where the fuck was he? Was he in the hospital or was he snorting an eight-ball of coke off of some chick's ass? Hint, he wasn't in the hospital. It wasn't an important gig, so we didn't make a huge deal of it, but it irrevocably affected me. Did I want to place my life, and my future, in Alex's hands? Only a few months later, my answer became clear. They say the world ends with a fizzle and not with a bang. My world fizzled out that night at Bobby's Tribeca bar. I just didn't know it yet.

Since back in The Reactions days, even if there were only ten people in the audience, we would still play to the best of our abilities. We just never knew if one of those ten people might be the one to discover us. I reminded my Circus of Power bandmates of this before every single performance. Turns out that Daniel Rey, a major NYC powerhouse record producer, had been at our Lismar Lounge shows, and liked what he saw. He contacted an A&R person from RCA, Wendy Goldstein, and suggested that she check us out. On July 4th, Circus of Power played The Hell's Angels block party on E. 3rd Street during the afternoon and Lismar Lounge, only a stone's throw away on 1st Avenue between E. 2nd and 3rd Streets, later that night. That's all that Wendy needed to see. We were offered a recording contract with RCA Records. Correction: **They** were offered a contract. I had quit the band the very next day, on July 5th. Alex couldn't believe that I could possibly be quitting on the eve of signing a record deal with a major record label. He tried to reason with me and then he pleaded with me. Not for his sake, 'cause I could be replaced, but for my own sake. He knew very well that I had been dreaming of getting a record deal since I was 14 years old. I stuck to my guns and told the band no thanks; they were on their own to negotiate a deal.

Circus of Power

This was huge! There was no possibility of ever returning to the music business if I walked away now. It was goodbye forever. The semester at Baruch College had finished, but I didn't have a degree yet. My job was a $10 per hour glorified handyman, so there was no career waiting for me on the other side. With all those factors working against me, one would think that my decision would be simple…stay with the band! But I thought it through intensely. This was the proverbial defining fork in the road. If I stayed with the band, there would be no turning back from that world. That ended up being accurately true. Circus of Power was singularly dedicated to playing music until the band broke up in 1994. They reached some incredible heights, which many times made me doubt, and even regret my decision. But when it was over, it was over. I would have been 32 years old then, with little chance for another career. My choices were to either bet on myself now or rely forever on Circus of Power. My decision boiled down to Alex deciding to snort coke off of a chick's ass rather than show up for a gig. I decided to bet on myself and informed the band that my decision was final.

Regrets…I've Had a Few

And so started a phase in my life that 30 years later, I'm still in. For 30 years, I have dedicated myself to helping individual investors manage their municipal bond portfolios. It's a great job that I love doing, and it has afforded me the opportunity to live a happy life in a nice house in Hollywood, Florida with my wife Robin and two daughters, Sophia and Reyna. But it certainly ain't rock and roll. The flipside of leaving the band was that they were now living the lifestyle that I had always wanted. They became rock stars and dealing with their success was just as difficult as advancing my own, challenging career. They remained my good friends, especially Ricky, and I wished them the best, but it was tough on me. When the first eponymously titled album came out, it was filled with material that I not only developed the drum parts for, but also helped shape and arrange the songs themselves. It was a fabulous album, but I couldn't help but wonder if it would have been even better had I stayed with the band. When the band broke up in 1994 after attaining great heights, I also couldn't help but wonder again. What if I had stayed with the band? Would we have stayed together?

On September 10th, 1988, I went to The Pier on W. 42nd Street and 12th Avenue in NYC for Circus of Power's first big gig opening up for Jane's Addiction and Iggy Pop. The first album had just been released and Ricky was reaping those nice perks that go along with success in rock. Gorgeous girls…models, fashion editors, and girls that looked as if they had stepped out of an MTV video, were all of a sudden falling over themselves to be with him. I, on the other hand, had gained 15 pounds from

Regrets...I've had a Few

being at my desk for too many hours a day, and had short, conservative hair. Those same girls, if they weren't looking through me, seemed annoyed by my presence. It required an effort on my part to maintain my self-esteem and to not get depressed. From time to time, it was too much for me to handle. That night at The Pier was one of those nights. Ricky gave Sonnie, Rose, and I tickets and vouchers for us to get into the concert and to drink for free. Watching Circus of Power play that night took a heavy toll on me. I used voucher after voucher to buy beers until the pain went away. It was a spectacular night for Circus of Power, but a depressing night for me.

I bottomed out only a few months later. Now that the record was out, Circus of Power's popularity was growing exponentially. Ricky was invited to dinner one Saturday night at The Old Homestead with Axl Rose of Guns N' Roses. I don't think it's necessary to mention, but I will anyway; Guns N' Roses has sold over 100 million records and at the time was the most popular band on earth. Ricky was having dinner with the singer of the band? Afterwards, Ricky met us at the Holiday Bar on St. Marks Place, which was our hangout of many years, and humbly didn't boast or make a big deal out of it. Quite the contrary. Undoubtedly sensitive to my feelings, he downplayed it by saying it was just a dinner. As interesting and exciting that my job on Wall Street was, the last few months had me really wondering if I had royally fucked up by not cashing in my winning band lottery ticket. The following night, Sunday, November 13th, 1988, my mental funk reached a crescendo. I met a few friends, including Gigo and his girlfriend Maria Ma, at The Idiot on 2nd Avenue and 12th Street, to enjoy a few cocktails before the weekend officially ended. The Idiot was a laid-back little bar in the East Village and the jukebox was exclusively country songs. It was not uncommon for Maria to end up behind the bar at one point or another, and by 10 p.m. was back there

Regrets...I've had a Few

pouring me triple shots of straight Jack Daniels. After a few rounds of drinking the Jack with evil intent, I shifted into a different gear and suggested that we should all walk over to The Ritz to go see the sold-out Jimmy Page show. I drunkenly proclaimed that I could get us all in, but nobody took it very seriously. Gigo and Maria went with me, but only because they were going home that way anyway. We got to the Ritz box office and the girl behind the glass told us that the show was sold out. I announced to her that I was Joey Wrecked, the drummer of Circus of Power. She leaned forward to take a better look at me and said, "You don't look like the drummer of Circus of Power." I sort of growled at her and then repeated loudly, "**I'm the drummer of Circus of Power. Let us in!**" She didn't need to deal with this kind of shit, and so she just said, "Ok, ok.... go on in then!" We walked into the VIP section in the balcony of The Ritz to watch Jimmy Page play, and I took up where I had left off in my quest to overdose on Jack Daniels. My head had been totally messed up the last few months, even causing Sonnie to temporarily kick me out of the Mulberry Street apartment. Tonight, I was crashing at my cousin Leon's apartment in Flushing, and so after the show, I took the short walk to the #5 train on Park Avenue South and 14th Street. Instead of heading north towards Grand Central Station, where I would then transfer to the #7 train, I somehow ended up southbound towards Brooklyn. Before I could get to the next exit to reverse my direction, I passed out.

A teenage kid, pointing a black revolver at me, awakened me at the very end of the #5 line. Two hours after talking my way into seeing Jimmy Page and Jason Bonham, I was at the dead end of a nasty and deserted subway station, on an empty, now out-of-service train, surrounded by a different type of band; a band of young criminals. There was a fucking gun shoved a few inches from my face. Five years ago, this was the same exact exit to my

Regrets...I've had a Few

cousin Sophie's house, and it had symbolized a new, exciting beginning. Now, as I was being held up at gunpoint, it was just the end of the line for me. The hoodlums kept asking me for my wallet, but I never gave it to them. I told them that there was no money in my wallet, which was true, and after a minute or two of threats and waiving the gun in my face, the leader, who was probably no older than 17 years old, gave me a friendly slap on the shoulder of my leather jacket and told me to take it easy. And then they were gone. It probably was incredibly dumb of me to try and win these guys over because who knows what they were thinking or what they were really willing to do. But somehow, I connected with them. Soon after they had filed out through the open doors, the train was back in service and headed back towards Manhattan. I passed out again almost immediately and didn't wake up till the train was way past Manhattan and all the way up into the Bronx. It was a long, horrible night. But we all need to bottom out before we can rise again. From that day on, I committed to focusing on my own life and my own career and to not allow myself to be paralyzed, or haunted, by any doubts or regrets. As much as humanly possible, I have remained true to that commitment.

My resolve was tested again only a few months later. For almost an entire week, Howard Stern went on and on about a band that was better than even Bon Jovi. Seriously, the #1 disc jockey in America was telling his listeners that he liked Circus of Power better than he liked Bon Jovi, who he said he was even friends with! I'm not saying that Circus of Power was ever better than Bon Jovi, but I almost crashed my car when I heard Howard Stern say it on the radio. He talked about Circus of Power everyday for almost a full week, and if you've ever heard Howard Stern, you know how colorful and how convincing he could be. Although I initially got that, "Oh no, here we go again!" sinking feeling, it was quickly replaced by a, "Hey, those

Regrets...I've had a Few

are my friends!" proud feeling. Same thing when the Tom Hanks movie, *The 'Burbs* came out. There's a scene in the movie where Corey Feldman plays the Circus of Power song "Machine" really loud on his front porch and plays air guitar to it. The music filled the entire movie theatre and it was fucking tremendous! I felt only happiness for my friends. Circus of Power was even mentioned on one of my favorite TV shows, *Beavis and Butt-Head*.

Again, it only made me proud.

My last serious bout with regret came many years later when I visited Ricky in Los Angeles in 1993, and he played for me the entire third album, *Magic and Madness*, before it had even been released to the public. Three massive rock stars, Ian Astbury of The Cult, Jerry Cantrell of Alice in Chains, and Gregg Bissonette, David Lee Roth's remarkably talented drummer, perform on it. Circus of Power was now signed to Columbia Records and the new record was magnificent. "Dreams Tonight," the song that I wrote all of the music to, was included on the album. Drummers often toil in obscurity and our names are difficult to find in the credits, if they are included at all. On some widely available bootleg Battalion of Saints records (such as *Best of the Battalion of Saints-Rock in Peace*), somebody else's name actually appears on the credits, even if I am the one actually doing the drumming. It therefore made me proud to see my name, J. Maya, listed as the co-songwriter of "Dreams Tonight," on Columbia Records no less. After listening to that phenomenal *Magic and Madness* with Ricky, I again had to consciously overcome that Pete Best feeling that enveloped me. As great as Circus of Power was and as loyal as their tens of thousands of fans were, the band broke up in 1994. Many factors contributed to the break up. I get a nagging feeling that if I had been around, some of those issues would not have even been there to begin with. It's obviously impossible to re-write history, but **what if** I had decided to give Alex a break?

Regrets...I've had a Few

After all, nobody's perfect, and we've all occasionally made some bad decisions. If I had stayed in Circus of Power, would Howard Stern's prophecy have come true and the band become bigger than Bon Jovi? Probably not, but we will obviously never know for sure. And that my friends, is what this life is all about.

Dreams Tonight

People come up to me all the time and tell me that since I'm a drummer, I must be a really good dancer. I wish they would add the word "good" before the word "drummer."

The truth is that I suck at dancing, but I'm pretty good at math. And that's mostly what drumming is, math.

Eventually, all good drummers realize that there are an infinite number of patterns possible to play on a drum kit, and that no matter how good you've become, you will only still be scratching the surface of those possibilities. In order to even come to that realization, the drummer will have undoubtedly already climbed many mountains and only now is becoming painfully aware that more remain to be conquered. But that's where the magic occurs, on those last series of mountains.

That's where Steve Gadd was able to turn the music of Steely Dan and Chick Corea into a showcase for his own virtuoso drumming and that's were he invented the creative, complex, and enduring drum licks for Paul Simon's "50 Ways To Leave Your Lover."

That's where Stewart Copeland, from The Police, can convert the complex math of drumming into the muscle memory that allows him to play whatever he wants, whenever he wants to.

Dreams Tonight

And that's where Larry Mullen, Jr., of U2, is able to come up with the razor sharp, machine-gun-like, sophisticated patterns that drive every U2 song.

It's more than just the strokes that are played. The strokes that are left out are just as important as those that are played. In reality, it is more difficult mentally and physically to leave strokes out. Led Zeppelin's John Bonham, one of the most effective and powerful rock drummers of all time, was a master of waiting, and waiting, and then **boom**, the perfect stroke. Listen to him again with that in mind. It's like comparing a chatty person to a person who talks less but chooses his words very carefully. John Bonham chose his strokes very carefully, and that's what made him such a great drummer.

That's what Doug Burris, the director of the Miami Beach Senior High Rock Ensemble was looking for at the Rock Ensemble audition that I miserably failed at many years ago. Mr. Burris wanted to see which drummers had the discipline to sound powerful, creative, and in control, while playing the difficult, molasses slow, 6/8 time signature. A typical way to play 6/8 time is to hit the snare drum twice and bass drum three times every six beats, and to do so while playing a very precise, equally spaced pattern on the ride cymbal. To me, that wasn't playing drums, that was **not playing** the drums. I was there to show him how good I was, not how fucking restrained I was. What I didn't know then was that they are one and the same. What you don't play is just as important as what you play.

Doug Burris suffered from the crippling disease Multiple Sclerosis and was partially paralyzed and in a wheelchair for 37 of the 40 years that he directed Rock Ensemble. That's 40 years of demanding and receiving perfection from his musician students, while he himself was very uncomfortable. Music motivated him

Dreams Tonight

to not only keep Rock Ensemble at its best, but to keep himself alive as well. What, other than music, could have possibly accomplished that for so long? Mr. Burris died in 2016 as I was finishing this book. Death demands that things be put into the proper perspective. I wish I had done so sooner.

When I was 14 years old, I was already a good enough basic drummer to play my first gig with a band called Eclipse at the La Gorce Country Club on Miami Beach. At the end of a particularly well-played set, a super cute, popular girl from my middle school came up to me and asked if I wanted to go smoke a joint with her on the golf course. I didn't go, but the lesson was crystal fucking clear; good music and good drumming equals hot girls that would normally be out of my reach.

Maybe that has always been my problem. Maybe the lesson wasn't as crystal clear as I thought it was. Maybe it was less about the girls and more about the craft.

Nahhhhhh. It was clear. She was hot!

I am still a drummer. And you know what they say about drummers.

I hope you enjoyed my story.

THE END

ACKNOWLEDGEMENTS

It's not always easy to be honest and polite at the same time. Rob Mittleman and Isaac Baruch, thank you for choosing honesty. My beta readers…. all great writers in their own right. Thank you Bob Suren, William Ashton, Jeff Lemlich, Todd Anthony, and Greg Baker. Aimee Heller, you went above and beyond. Thank you for the nudge in the right direction. My fellow Jitney drivers, Abel Folgar and David Rolland, thanks for catching those (hopefully) last pesky mistakes. Brad Meltzer, Bruce Turkel, Rochelle Berger Weinstein, and Steven Blush, I promise to pay it forward.

My smart brother Isaac, whether it was hooking me up on Word or that golden nugget of an expression, this task would have been much, much more difficult without your help.

All my friends that helped me remember, I couldn't have pieced this story together without you.

To my publisher, J.J. Colagrande, thank you for fighting to give anti-corporate, anti-social, South Florida rebels like me a chance to be heard. We need more publishers like Jitney Books!

My wife and kids, Robin, Sophia, and Reyna, oh my God, thank you for putting up with me while I wrote this book…it could not have been easy! All I do is for you.

Finally, to Joey Wrecked. Yes, he is real…unless you are law enforcement or my daughters. In that case, purely fictional!

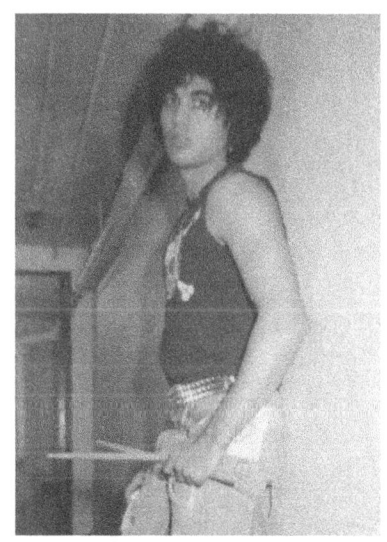

Joey Wrecked

www.ingramcontent.com/pod-product-compliance
Lightning Source LLC
Chambersburg PA
CBHW022102090426
42743CB00008B/685